Teen Anger Management Education

Implementation Guidelines for Counselors

Eva L. Feindler • Gina Sita-Molz

LIBRARY OF
CONGRESS
SURPLUS
DUPLICATE

RESEARCH PRESS
PUBLISHERS

Champaign, Illinois ▪ [800] 519-2707 ▪ www.researchpress.com

RESEARCH PRESS
PUBLISHERS

Copyright © 2021 by Eva L. Feindler and Gina Sita-Molz

5 4 3 2 1   21 22 23 24 25

All rights reserved. Printed in the United States of America.

Handouts and worksheets with publication citation on the bottom of the page may be reproduced for educational classroom use by the original purchaser only.

All handouts and worksheets are available to the purchaser
from the publisher's website at **www.researchpress.com/downloads**

No other parts of this book may be reproduced by any means without the written permission of the publisher. Excerpts may be printed in connection with published reviews in periodicals without express permission.

Copies of this book may be ordered from the publisher at www.researchpress.com.

Composition by Jeff Helgesen
Printed by Seaway Printing Co.

ISBN 978-0-87822-729-7
LOC 2020943415

I want to thank my family for their continued support across my career and travels to bring the TAME approach to other states and other countries. In particular, I want to dedicate this volume to my mother, Joan LaGarde Feindler, for her inspiration in finding a career in therapy and teaching that I love and which has given my life such deep meaning. I still miss her every day.

—Eva L. Feindler

I am extremely grateful to my parents for their love, care, and sacrifices. Thank you for instilling a love of learning from an early age and providing the emotional and financial support to allow me to pursue my career aspirations. Also, I am very thankful to my husband and children for their love, understanding, and continuing support to complete this book.

—Gina Sita-Molz

Contents

Acknowledgments

I am deeply indebted to all who have worked with me over the years that I have been involved with the development of anger management programs for children and their families. My first mentor, Dr. Arnie Goldstein, was truly a pioneer, and we worked together on many different projects—many published by Research Press—until his untimely death in 2002. I will never forget his wisdom and his desire to share our skills-training approaches with everyone who might benefit. My association with him led to a longtime affiliation with his international supporters of aggression replacement training (the talented folks from Canada, Sweden, and Norway): Knut Gunderson, Robert Calame, Garbis Sarafian, Rune Nensén, and Bengt Daleflod. I will always treasure my travels and our global training programs in anger management.

I am also deeply grateful for the collaborations with many graduate students over the years as we transformed our training into the current TAME model. In particular, I want to thank Meghann Gerber, Emily Engel, Kristen Byrnes, and Alex Mercurio. And, of course, I am so thankful for my coauthor, Gina Sita-Molz, who has become a valued colleague through our collaboration.

—Eva L. Feindler

I would like to express my sincere gratitude to my coauthor and advisor, Dr. Eva Feindler. Thank you for providing support and invaluable guidance throughout the dissertation process. It was a great privilege and honor to work and study under your leadership. Since this book includes my dissertation research, I would also like to thank the rest of my research committee: Dr. David Roll and Dr. Jennifer Jablonski. You served as important mentors throughout my education, providing your direct advice and acting as positive models for professional development. I appreciate your encouragement, insightful comments, and thoughtful questions.

—Gina Sita-Molz

Introduction

Based upon a long tradition of anger management interventions and the evidence base, *Teen Anger Management Education: Implementation Guidelines for Counselors* was developed. This book is for mental health professionals and educators who continue their efforts to help angry and aggressive teens learn better emotion management and interpersonal skills. A brief overview of each of the chapters follows.

Chapter 1—Foundations for TAME: Theory and Research

Following a general update on current understandings in the clinical literature on youth anger, youth aggression, and contextual factors, we review recent interventions related to anger management for youth. Enhanced, effective interventions for angry youth require a better integration of emotion regulation skills training. Definitions, an articulation of adaptive strategies, and a discussion of maladaptive strategies often associated with aggression follow.

Chapter 2—Assessment Measures and Strategies

This is a short and practical discussion on the need for the assessment of individual and program outcomes. Included is a review of a number of useful self-report inventories and parent/teacher inventories, as well as self-monitoring methods that TAME leaders might find helpful in program data collection.

Chapter 3—Preparation for TAME: Planning for Program Implementation

This chapter presents an overview of the revised version of TAME, a 12-session comprehensive skills training focused on the regulation of anger and the development of self-control and healthy interpersonal functioning. Issues to consider when preparing for the implementation of a TAME program are reviewed. Individual variables associated with better outcomes, as well as actual case examples from groups, are discussed.

Chapter 4—TAME Session-by-Session Protocol

This chapter hosts descriptions of each session, including content layout, training goals, in-session exercises, and homework assignments. Relevant activities and worksheets are also included. The manual has been updated to remain culturally relevant for today's teen; for example, aspects of relational aggression are integrated into discussion concerning technology and current aspects of social media communication. New developments in research and assessment are reflected in changes to the program manual.

Chapter 5—Implementation Issues and Recommendations

In this chapter, strategies for planning a successful TAME intervention program and issues relative to staffing and supervision are presented. Suggestions for individual applications of the TAME manual and tips for implementation in schools, agencies, and residential placements are provided.

Chapter 6—Initial Evaluation of TAME in a Middle School Setting

This is a brief description of the implementation and evaluation of a coed-group TAME program in a middle school. Changes on several assessment measures provide initial evidence for the efficacy of the intervention. Included in this chapter are the four tables from this initial program evaluation of TAME in a middle school.

Appendixes and References

These sections include resources for other materials; program handouts for parents, teachers, and teens; homework and self-monitoring sheets; in-session worksheets; and references. There is at least one worksheet and a fidelity checklist for every session so that the desired implementation approach to TAME can be monitored. Also included are additional mindfulness exercises for use throughout the TAME program.

Section One

Chapter 1

Foundations for TAME: Theory and Research

Although there has been tremendous growth in intervention approaches for youth with externalizing behavior problems, anger and the aggression that sometimes accompanies it continue to be of significant concern for mental health professionals and others who work with such youth. This complex category of emotional and behavioral symptoms has been represented by the diagnostic categories in *DSM-IV* of oppositional defiant disorder, conduct disorder, and intermittent explosive disorder (American Psychiatric Association [APA], 2000). A recent suggestion, based on a sample of over 4,000 children whose parents completed the Swanson, Nolan, and Pelham (SNAP) questionnaire, is that oppositional defiant disorder is better understood as a disorder of emotion regulation, while conduct disorder captures defiant and aggressive behavior patterns. In the latest version, *DSM-5*, the diagnostic category of disruptive mood dysregulation disorder, included within the category for depressive disorders, is used for youth with severe chronic irritability accompanied by frequent temper outbursts. The first diagnostic criterion is severe recurrent temper outbursts manifested verbally (e.g., verbal rages) and/or behaviorally (e.g., physical aggression toward people or property) that are grossly out of proportion in intensity or duration to the situation or provocation (APA, 2013). Due both to the newness of this categorization and to questions about the reliability and validity of this diagnosis, it is hard to estimate the prevalence of this symptom presentation. It is anticipated that these "naughty, grumpy" children and adolescents will be common referrals to mental health clinics. APA (2013) suggests that what research exists indicates that disruptive mood dysregulation disorder is more frequent in males; as with all disorders, significant impairment must exist in several settings to meet criteria.

Counselors, school professionals, teachers, and certainly parents still seek effective prevention and intervention strategies for assisting youth in navigating the typically occurring emotion of anger while achieving healthy personal and interpersonal outcomes. The following review of current research findings on emotion regulation and dysregulation, as well as on contextual influences, helps to frame the proposed Teen Anger Management Education (TAME) program described in detail in Chapter 3.

Emotion Regulation

Over the past decade, there has been an explosion in research on emotion regulation (ER) and dysregulation—particularly in the regulation of anger. Some have proposed developing a better understanding of the normal development of emotion regulation competence, which helps then to define the deficits that youth with externalizing behavior problems might have. McLaughlin et al. (2011) described the typical developmental progression for learning adaptive emotion regulation skills: First, there is the development of emotion awareness and understanding with a finer discrimination between emotions. Next, there is the development of a variety of emotional expressions, both nonverbal and verbal. Finally, at a later stage, there is the development of cognitive emotion regulation strategies. Here, the child engages in specific thoughts or behaviors in response to emotional experiences in an attempt to manage or reduce the negative affect and achieve goals (McLaughlin et al., 2011). Development of emotion regulation strategy use involves a transition from reliance on suppression during childhood to greater use of reappraisal in adolescence and adulthood—a transition that parallels developmental changes in executive functions (Lantrip et al., 2016). Although Lantrip's research was not with a clinical sample ($n = 70$), results indicated that greater reliance on the use of reappraisal was associated with fewer difficulties with emotion control (e.g., fewer outbursts, greater stability) and with behavior regulation more generally. Trends were also observed for reappraisal to be related to better inhibitory control and executive functioning in general. According to Röll et al. (2012), most children develop strategies to cope with their emotions and manage their behavior in demanding situations. However, children who show an early onset of high levels of externalizing behavior may not acquire more effective regulatory strategies.

In general, ER refers to attempts an individual makes to maintain, inhibit, and/or enhance emotional experience and expression. There has been an increased recognition that the regulation of emotions is necessary for healthy psychological development. According to Gullone et al. (2010), ER includes intrinsic and extrinsic processes responsible for managing one's emotions toward goal accomplishment. ER processes can be conscious or unconscious and include skills for monitoring, evaluating, and modifying both positive and negative emotional reactions. Also included are ER strategies for reducing the intensity or frequency of emotional states and capacities to generate and sustain emotions. Typically, ER strategies are aligned along the following adaptive/maladaptive continuum and are best used in a flexible fashion according to situational variables:

- Adaptive strategies associated with greater psychological health:
    - *Emotional awareness*: understanding and clarity of emotional responses, ability to recognize and describe internal emotional experiences.
    - *Emotional acceptance*: nonjudgmental experience of both positive and negative emotions.
    - Access to a variety of adaptive emotion regulation responses that incorporate modulation of both internal experiences and external responses that are (a) appropriate to the situation and (b) conducive to goal attainment. These will include:
        - *Problem solving*: "What are the goals? Where am I heading?"
        - *Cognitive reappraisal*: most researched strategy in Gross's (2002) model of ER; redefines a potentially emotion-eliciting situation in such a way that the emotional impact is changed.
        - *Decentering*: capacity to take a detached view of one's thoughts and emotions. "Self as process." Cognitive diffusion or distancing developed from the acceptance and commitment therapy's focus along the dimensions of social, temporal, spatial, and experiential distance.
- Maladaptive strategies more often associated with aggression and anger:
    - *Underregulation* represents a failure to contain difficult emotional experiences or to inhibit impulsive behaviors. High levels of physiological arousal, which accompanies intense affects, impede information processing, which then precludes the implementation of more adaptive ER strategies. Sometimes this is manifested in a venting or "spreading activation" when one negative affect leads to another, then leads to another, and so on.
    - *Overregulation* captures efforts to stop emotions from unfolding and/or being expressed.

- Emotional and experiential avoidance strategies are typically rigid and inflexible efforts to escape from or avoid unpleasant internal experiences and any circumstances that might trigger them (Eifert & Forsyth, 2011).

- *Expressive suppression*: The second most researched strategy from Gross's (2002) initial ER model is expressive suppression, a type of inhibition when one hides signs of anger.

- *Rumination*: Rumination/dwelling, described as the replaying of the anger-provoking situation, predicts aggression above and beyond the experience of anger. Deliberate replaying and rehearsing acts of revenge intensifies anger, and past and future events dominate.

- *Cognitive fusion*: This is the tendency for behavior to be overly regulated and influenced by thoughts. Cognitive events dominate behavior and experience over other sources of information (Gillander et al., 2014), and these events cannot be viewed from any other perspective. Thoughts are taken as truth, and the individual becomes entangled in and dominated by those distorted thoughts.

Much of the developmental research has focused on young children and their parents. Ideally, parents serve as good role models and "coaches" for the development of healthy, adaptive regulation strategies. Katz et al. (2012) suggested a parent metaemotion hypothesis indicating that parents' beliefs, thoughts, and attitudes guide their own emotion processing and their responses to their children; thus it might follow that parents who have adaptive ER skills will know how to teach their children emotion awareness, acceptance, and expression. Gullone et al. (2010) examined the normative development of emotion regulation strategies in a large community sample across 2 years. Administering the Emotion Regulation Questionnaire for Children and Adolescents (ERQ-CA) at three different times, girls and older children reported less use of suppression strategies, whereas older boys and girls reported less use of cognitive appraisal strategies. This unexpected result may indicate that ER strategies may not be linear across development. Although the research on adaptive and maladaptive emotion regulation with children and adolescents is very limited, there is much to be learned from research conducted with angry and aggressive adults.

Research on ER and aggression has been focused on dysregulated anger. Herts et al. (2012) examined emotion dysregulation as a potential mechanism linking stressful experiences to aggressive behavior in a large ($n = 1,065$) sample of early adolescents. Results from this longitudinal study indicated that dysregulated emotional reactivity leads to heightened sensitivity to emotional cues, which then increases the likelihood of aggressive responding. Röll et al. (2012) reviewed longitudinal studies that examined the relationship between emotion regulation and aggressive/externalizing behavior in childhood and suggested that emotion dysregulation in children is clearly associated with externalizing problems like aggression and therefore constitutes an important risk factor.

Lately, there has been much more focus on the subtypes (relational, reactive, and proactive) of aggression in youth bullying and peer victimization. *Reactive aggression* is defined as impulsive and angry responses to perceived provocation or threat. *Proactive aggression* represents a more planned and premeditated aggression that is goal-directed for either instrumental gain or dominance over others. There are several key differences between these two groups in terms of cognitive and emotional factors. Youth exhibiting reactive aggression often have low frustration tolerance, poor emotion regulation, and a cognitive distortion to attribute hostile intent to others' actions. Those exhibiting proactive aggression have a more minimized emotional response to cues, evidence belief in the use of aggression to reach goals, and seem to show a lack of guilt or empathy (often labeled as Callous-Unemotional traits). Interestingly, emotion recognition training results in increased affective empathy and reduction in conduct problems for children with Callous-Unemotional traits (Dadds et al., 2012).

Relational aggression has been a more recent focus and is more frequent in females. This is typified by harm to relationships exhibited by, perhaps, spreading rumors, social exclusion, lies, and gossip. Relational aggression emerges in childhood but peaks during adolescence upon attainment of developmental milestones such as increased verbal capacities, more extensive social relationships, and the ability to understand others' mental states and then to know better how to harm the relationship (Voulgaridou & Kokkinos, 2015). Finally, *bullying* can be defined as aggression specifically—and therefore more intentionally—toward someone perceived as weaker or less able to defend themselves. Other research (Crapanzano et al., 2010) has shown that there are two distinct groups of youth: those with reactive aggression only and those with both proactive and reactive. The latter group has more severe behavioral and emotional disturbances and shows the highest rates of bullying. In sum, relational, reactive, and proactive aggressive-behavior patterns are most likely accompanied by differing patterns of emotion regulation strategies as well as differing aspects of cognitive appraisals. These patterns will need consideration in any effective anger management treatment approach for youth.

Consideration of Context

Many advancements in our understanding of family development and dynamics will help to inform the next wave of effective psychosocial interventions for acting-out youth. In particular, clinical research has helped us to understand the impact of parental psychopathology on the functioning of developing children. Research by Bariola et al. (2012) provides evidence for the intergenerational transmission of emotion regulation strategies and dysfunction.

Parents who have significant emotional disorders have altered perceptions of their children and choose ineffective and sometimes harsher discipline strategies. It is logical that the emotional disturbances evidenced by certain parents will directly and at times significantly impact the attachment processes so critical to parent–child functioning. Parental emotion dysregulation has a significant impact on family functioning: A traditional style of harsh, authoritarian parenting is often and unpredictably accompanied by explosive and anger-driven parenting, the consequences of which can devastate the child's sense of self-competency and relationship functioning.

In response, many more parent-training professionals have adapted their evidence-based programs (PCIT and Triple P, for example) to target parental emotion regulation. This approach helps to secure better models for children developing emotion regulation skills and to teach parents more effective approaches for responding to their child's anger displays and aggressive responding. In 2005, Dumas described a model of mindfulness-based parent training (MBPT) for parents of disruptive children. MBPT is based on behavioral parent training with a special focus on bringing automatic, mindless behavior into awareness in order to decrease maladaptive parent–child interactions. Mindful parenting interventions may be particularly helpful for parents of children with behavioral difficulties. A later model proposed by Duncan et al. (2009) targets five key parenting dimensions: listening with full attention, nonjudgmental acceptance of child and self, emotional awareness of self and child, self-regulation in the parenting relationship, and compassion for the child and self. Successful implementation of mindful parenting has been shown to increase effective parenting, reduce discipline accompanied by intense negative affect, and lead to improved parent–child relationships (Duncan et al., 2009).

Bögels et al. (2008) reported on eight sessions of group mindfulness training for parents and adolescents with externalizing disorders. After mindfulness training, young adolescents self-reported substantial improvement on personal goals, internalizing and externalizing complaints, attention problems, happiness, and mindful awareness. Parents reported improvement on children's behaviors, self-control, attunement to others, and withdrawal; however, neither parent ER nor parent mindfulness was assessed. Further, an adaptation of *Strengthening Our Families*, with the addition of mindfulness training, was reported by Coatsworth et al. (2010). These authors suggest that the transition to adolescence is one of the most challenging for parents and teen, especially when there are long-established patterns of negative and coercive interactions.

What have not yet received sufficient attention are parent-training programs designed for parents of angry and aggressive adolescents. Family TAME might be the best next adaptation of the anger management skills training described in this book. However, the combination of all dysregulated family members working session-to-session while the family dynamics prevail might be too difficult to implement. A unique 8-week, 6-step integrative intervention to address parents' and adolescents' deficits in affect regulation and attachment based on principles of emotionally focused therapy (EFT) and multidimensional family therapy (MDFT) for incarcerated teens was described by Keiley (2002). For 3 weeks, the parent group and the adolescent group met separately to discuss videos of interpersonal family conflict and resolution strategies. The remaining sessions were conducted with multiple families together, which might help to stem the dynamics that each family brings to therapy. Via role play and thought records, all participants learned emotion management for cycles of anger and acting out toward the other. Healthier attachment was facilitated by perspective taking and communicating vulnerabilities. The creators of this approach reported improvements and satisfaction for the participants but also commented on the obstacles presented by the context of implementation in correctional facilities and the general resistance to change that parents have in regard to their own behavior (Keiley, 2002). Future adaptations to other contexts are hoped for. The blending of anger management strategies and family interventions is an appealing way to ensure that changes in affect regulation for adolescents are maintained after an intervention program is completed.

Understanding of Anger and Aggression Disorders

Along with consideration of the development of emotion regulation and the role played by family, research on the relationship of anger to other emotions and diagnostic categories has helped to inform intervention planning for youth with externalizing behavior problems. There are several comorbidity issues that need to be addressed in anger management programs. Often, anger is associated with sadness and shame, which may trigger patterns of avoidance and withdrawal. According to available research, anger dysregulation can accompany other diagnostic categories of depressive disorder and social anxiety. The recent *DSM-5* designation for disruptive mood dysregulation disorder for youth is included as an aspect of the depressive disorders.

Anger dysfunction is also related to personality disorders and delinquency. The research from Paul Frick and colleagues on the development and evocation of Callous-Unemotional traits in children and adolescents has helped us to understand key cognitive distortions and deficits that will impair the development of empathy and the ability to relate to others in a healthy way. Oppositional defiant disorder and conduct disorder criteria emphasize ongoing patterns of an angry or irritable mood, defiant or argumentative behavior, and vindictiveness toward people in authority. Generally, these behavior patterns occur in early childhood and must be evaluated in the context of the child's developmental level. There is significant comorbidity in the externalizing behavior disorders' presentations such that youth referred for anger management due to a lack of emotional control also have significant attentional problems. This will create the need for careful planning of interventions for those with ADHD.

Some researchers have suggested that perhaps there are common mechanisms (Gratz et al., 2015) that connect emotional dysregulation patterns in general, leading to difficulties in distinguishing between emotional presentations. In fact, the usual emotion regulation strategies that are employed universally by children and adults (e.g., reappraisal, suppression, concealing) are effective for many of the negative emotions. Others have suggested patterns of cognitive and emotional distortions that are cyclical and feed one another. Anger ruminations leading to shame, thoughts of revenge, and continued focus on the source and blame for conflict (Denson et al., 2012; White & Turner, 2014) perpetuate an internal justification for a revenge response. A corollary area of research is on the development and deficits in self-regulation capacity as a set of universal skills applicable to emotion regulation.

In fact, Berking's recent volume on affect regulation training (ART; Berking & Lukas, 2015) is an approach to teaching a set of universal skills for emotion regulation for adults. This transdiagnostic approach, rooted in emotion science and theory, has also been exemplified in the adult literature *Unified Protocol for Treatment of Emotional Disorder* (Barlow et al., 2010). The Unified Protocol (UP) consists of four core modules: increasing emotional awareness, facilitating flexibility in appraisals, identifying and preventing behavioral and emotional avoidance, and situational and interoceptive exposure to emotion cues (Ellard et al., 2010). Ample clinical research supports the effectiveness of the UP for adults with a variety/heterogeneity of disorders. There is some research (Ehrenreich et al.,

2009) on the development and initial research support for individual treatment of adolescents that targets negative emotionality and associated psychological difficulties—particularly anxiety and depressive disorders. This fills a need for novel and effective treatment approaches that target commonalities in emotional disorder symptom presentation and their intervention. Certainly, this type of intervention may be more efficient and may have significant implications for healthier emotional development for youth; however, further research, with larger sample sizes of adolescents and across clinical contexts, is still necessary.

Recent Developments in Anger Management Interventions for Youth

Lately, there have been some innovative treatment programs and protocols reported in the literature that focus on youth with anger and aggression difficulties. The following review of highlights from these approaches will frame some of the expansion of the TAME manual in Chapter 3.

- **Mode Deactivation Therapy (MDT)**: This empirically based treatment for angry and aggressive adolescents includes aspects of the "third wave" of cognitive behavioral therapy (CBT) treatments: acceptance and commitment therapy, mindfulness, and dialectical behavior therapy (DBT). MDT expanded mindfulness training to include a wider variety of mindfulness skills that adolescents could learn more quickly and easily than meditation, while adapting the DBT principles of validation and radical acceptance into its distinctive procedure of "validation, clarification, and redirection" (VCR). At the same time, MDT shares mindfulness and acceptance concepts with acceptance and commitment therapy and drew from some of its principles (such as cognitive diffusion). The youth who best benefit from this therapy are those who are to be considered to be emotionally charged, have maladaptive behaviors, and "fly off the handle" (get enraged or angry) too quickly in reaction to perceived threats. MDT utilizes mindfulness techniques to help improve self-regulation. Mindfulness is described in MDT as one being fully aware and accepting oneself as one is in the moment, without judgment (Bayles et al., 2014). The concept unique to the MDT methodology, known as VCR, is used to provide the adolescent with tools and guidance to find their own unconditional acceptance and validate their learning experience and may be the most pivotal component (Apsche et al., 2011). A recent meta-analysis of 21 outcome studies with 573 male adolescents with conduct and oppositional defiant disorders found a robust therapeutic model of care for adolescents who have extensive abuse histories, have been in multiple placements, and generally are avoided by providers due to their extreme behavior. MDT treatment may represent the best approach for adolescent males who exhibit extreme anger and aggression, but adaptations for girls and an understanding of how individual mental health providers can implement aspects remain to be seen.

- **Student Created Aggression Replacement Education (SCARE)** was developed in the 1990s with input from students themselves and was meant for broad implementation in a school setting. After asking students how to reduce violence in their schools, via essays that were then analyzed for content (a unique approach to needs assessment), ideas and strategies were blended with the empirical and clinical best practices. The 15-session program emphasized three primary areas: recognizing anger and violence in the community, managing and reducing self-expressions of anger, and defusing anger and violence in others. The last section was an expansion of anger management, as youth were encouraged to prevent violence and to learn how to promote peaceful resolution of conflict—more of a community approach than an individual clinical one. Bundy et al. (2011) evaluated the impact of booster sessions on maintaining intervention gains, and results confirmed this strategy. (See Herrmann and McWhirter, 2003, for a review of each session and a discussion of the program's effectiveness.) SCARE is one component of the GOPEP school prevention program described below.

- **Juvenile Justice Anger Management for Girls (JJAM)** began with an initial adaptation of the Lochman and Wells (2002) Coping Power program to meet the unique needs of adolescent girls housed in residential juvenile justice facilities. The gender-specific adaptations included greater emphasis on relationship skill building and relational aggression (e.g., spreading rumors, excluding others from activities, ending friendships) more likely exhibited by girls. Research has shown that girls' aggression—verbal, physical, and relational—tends to be associated with conflictual interpersonal relationships; Goldstein et al. (2013) provided an overview of the 16-session manualized treatment that is specific to the context of girls' residential treatment and typically structured with strategies of appraisal change process, emotion regulation, and problem solving. The authors have completed an RCT to determine program outcomes when compared to TAU and have examined the feasibility and acceptability of JJAM for girls in postadjudication programs (Goldstein et al., 2018). Results revealed greater reductions in anger, reactive physical aggression, and reactive relational aggression for the 57 girls in the JJAM treatment condition when compared with the TAU condition and when changes in hostile attribution bias were identified as a significant mechanism of action.

- **ACT with *RAGE-Control***: An active biofeedback video game (Ducharme et al., 2012) for practicing emotion regulation skills is called *RAGE-Control* (Regulate and Gain Emotional Control) and is CBT modified with anger control training (ACT). *RAGE-Control* is a video game intended to enhance players' abilities to regulate their emotions by challenging players to control their level of physiological arousal while remaining alert and responsive to the stress presented by the fast-paced challenges of a virtual environment. Designed to enhance self-regulatory capacities, it was evaluated for a single case of a 16-year-old girl with intensive implementation in a short-term psychiatric setting. The ACT with *RAGE-Control* intervention includes (a) psychoeducation about anger and aggression, (b) skill development to reduce feelings of anger, and (c) skill practice through overcoming simulated stress. The use of a video game and a virtual environment for the practice of emotion regulation skills is quite unique and shows promise given the technological interests of teens. Furthermore, there has been more of a focus on providing effective intervention service for youth via a group modality, which validates the relational priorities of adolescence and harnesses the group process for motivation to change.

- **The Violence Reduction Training Program (VRTP)** is a group-based intervention for court-ordered adults convicted of violent offenses (Gerhart et al., 2015), such as assault and domestic violence, that targets both frustration-aggression reactions and social problem solving deficits. The 13-session program, beginning with motivational interviewing strategies to elicit increased readiness to change, allows the conflict that eventually occurs in the group dynamics to function as an in vivo learning laboratory. Participants learn to challenge one another and work toward resolution and greater understanding of one another. For adolescents, the group dynamics might function similarly unless they all know one another already, as is the case in educational and congregate-care settings. Although promising, this group-process approach requires strong leadership to manage anger evoked in session.

- **Leadership Development**: Burt et al. (2012) reported on a creative intervention for increasing social and relational competencies of aggressive high school students. This anger management group was focused on creating leadership abilities and was advertised as such, although the participants chosen for the intervention were considered "at risk." The 12-week program included four themes: intentionality, forethought, self-reactiveness, and self-reflectiveness. Included were skills similar to self-regulation, problem solving, goal-directed behavior, and emotion regulation skills included in most anger management programs. With a small sample ($n = 32$) across four schools, a program evaluation indicated a reduction in anger and an increase in leadership skills. The authors suggested that leadership empowers teens and increases their sense of self-efficacy and that such a strengths-based program has greater appeal to a population of often treatment-resistant youth.

- **Group Oriented Psychoeducation Prevention (GOPEP)** is a large-scale school program for the prevention of violence (McWhirter & McWhirter, 2010). There are four specific components: SCARE (described above), SOAR (Student Optimistic Attitudes and Resiliency), BLOCKS (Building Lives on Companion Knowledge Skills), and ART (anxiety reduction training). This multitheoretical and multimodal program is ideal for implementation in education settings with a comprehensive curriculum guide. The GOPEP approach uses group processes to reduce future problems and to promote well-being and positive mental health of youth across community and school settings.

The latest research by Lochman and colleagues Muratori et al. (2015) reported longitudinal research on group-versus-individual Coping Power treatment for a large sample of fourth-grade children. Results indicated that both conditions reduced externalizing behavior problems reported by teachers and parents; however, for children with low initial levels of self-regulation, individual treatment yielded better outcomes. Although this research needs replication with an adolescent sample—since developmentally, the impact of the peer group is much different—both modalities of this evidenced-based approach have positive outcomes.

Summary: The Next Wave of Anger Management Interventions

This relatively brief review of the literature, with a focus on cognitive behavioral skills training for youth with externalizing behavior problems, centered on the development of emotion regulation strategies and emotion dysregulation aspects of problems of anger and aggression. Most psychoeducational skills programs for children and adolescents presenting with emotional disorders now include training in affect regulation and mindfulness. The typical psychoeducation skills-training programs can be enhanced by greater focus on self-awareness, validation of experiences and beliefs, and a more balanced approach to decision making in anger-arousing situations. There is a wider lens of application of anger management intervention across emotional disorders and diagnostic criteria. Based upon some research that suggests gender differences in negative emotional functioning and the accompanying behavioral disturbances, there are specific approaches that have been developed for girls

(Goldstein et al., 2013; Leve et al., 2015). There is convincing evidence that risky romantic relationships are the nexus of continued aggressive behavior and poor mental health among at-risk adolescent girls: Results show that these girls are victimized in their close relationships, and, in turn, they perpetuate aggression within their romantic relationships (Moretti et al., 2011). Future applications of anger management will likely include more specific gender and cultural modifications to increase sensitivities to the variations of the population.

Angry adolescents may or may not present with aggressive-behavior problems, which in most contexts comes to the attention of mental health professionals. What is known in the clinical circles is that this is the adolescent population most in need of intervention and yet the most resistant to intervention. Angry youth are often remanded to treatment services once they have broken enough rules—and perhaps the law. Involuntary youth are often unresponsive to traditional clinical intervention, and much can be gleaned from the literature on stages of change and motivational interviewing. Providers would be best served if they assessed the adolescent's stage of change and incorporated some motivational interviewing strategies invoked for hard-to-reach adult clients. *Stages of change* refers to a sequence of stages people go through on their way to making significant changes: (a) precontemplation, (b) contemplation, (c) preparation, (d) action, and (e) maintenance (Norcross et al., 2011). However, except for eating disorders, smoking, and substance abuse, this process has not been examined relative to youth externalizing problems. Linked to readiness to change, motivational interviewing has long been established as a process for helping individuals overcome resistance and explore motivations for changing behavior patterns. Research has reported effectiveness for adolescent health-related issues as well as substance use.

Most anger management intervention programs for youth are presented in a group format, although individualized treatment protocols can easily be extracted. Lately, there has also been increased emphasis on contextual factors, and programs have been reported in a variety of settings such as schools, community agencies, and correctional facilities. Most important is an increased focus on parents and family functioning. Parent training nowadays usually includes a mindfulness-training component in order to help parents understand their own emotional reactivity and reduce negative parent–child interactions. Research evidence supports this approach to more effective parenting and, hopefully, a better development of children's emotional regulation. The inclusion of parents in interventions for youth in juvenile justice settings seems imperative for long-term maintenance of treatment gains.

Chapter 2

Assessment Measures and Strategies

Assessment of Anger

Self-Report

Attitudes Toward Anger Management Scale (ATAMS) (Boudreaux et al., 2014): This is a 13-item self-report that is focused on attitudes toward seeking professional help with one's anger. Items center on two dimensions: Belief in Treatment (nine items: e.g., "If anger problems have lasted over a long period of time, anger management is a good idea") and Receptiveness (four items: e.g., "Given enough time, anger problems will solve themselves").

Anger Regulation and Expression Scale (ARES) (DiGiuseppe & Tafrate, 2011): This is a self-report measure of anger expression and regulation for youth aged 10 to 17 years. The 75 items are presented with statements regarding situations in which the youth might feel anger. A 5-point Likert-type scale from *never* to *always* is used to rate each item. Internal consistency was measured by calculating Cronbach's alpha across age and gender groups. Total alpha scores ranged from .97 to .99, and cluster-score values ranged from .87 to .97, revealing strong internal consistency. Test–retest reliability values ranged from $r = .58$ to $r = .92$ and were found to be significant ($p < .001$). A youth sample from the population that completed the ARES also completed either the Conners Comprehensive Behavior Rating Scales (Conners CBRS) and/or the Jesness Inventory–Revised (JI-R). The correlation between the total score of the ARES and the Conners CBRS was very strong with correlation coefficients between $r = .64$ and .70. The selected JI-R scores correlated with ARES scores ranged from moderate to strong with correlation coefficients between $r = .42$ and .52 for the total score, indicating strong convergent validity (Cavlazoglu et al., 2013).

State-Trait Anger Expression Inventory for Children and Adolescents (STAXI-CA) (del Barrio et al., 2004): The STAXI-CA was constructed adapting the STAXI-for-adults items to children and adolescents (ages 7–17) for a total of 45 items: 11 for State Anger (Part 1), 10 for Trait Anger (Part 2), and 24 for the different sorts of Anger Expression (Part 3; six for Anger Out and 13 for Anger Control). There is a Spanish version available as well. Good internal reliability and convergent and discriminant validity have all been reported.

Multidimensional School Anger Inventory (MSAI) (Smith et al., 1998): This self-report instrument, featuring 39 items, is designed to measure cognitive, behavioral, and affective dimensions of anger in the context of a school setting. The scale has positive psychometric properties with respect to construct validity and reliability. The four subscales are School Anger Experience Index (13 items), School Cynicism Index (hostile outlook), School Anger Expression Index (positive coping), and School Anger Expression Index (destructive expression). The MSAI has been examined with several groups of adolescents, the largest group (used for establishing psychometric properties) consisting of 1,589 high school students in Grades 9 through 12 (Furlong et al., 2002). Fifty percent of the sample was female, and although originally designed for male adolescents, it was found that the four-factor structure was replicated for females, with the Anger Experience subscale having the highest alpha coefficient: .83. In addition, a cross-validation analysis was completed with nonoverlapping subsamples of male and female students, which revealed an alpha coefficient of .84 for the Anger Experience subscale. In the initial instrument evaluation, the MSAI was found to have good internal consistency, with the Anger Experience subscale having the highest alpha coefficients across three samples, ranging .84 to .88 (Smith et al., 1998). Convergent validity was established via comparison with the Aggression Questionnaire (Buss & Warren, 2000) and the Conners Teacher Rating Scale (Conners, 1969).

Reactive-Proactive Aggression Questionnaire (R-PAQ) (Raine et al., 2006): The R-PAQ consists of 23 items rated on a 3-point Likert-type scale ranging from 0 (*never*) to 2 (*always*), assessing Reactive Aggression (e.g., "reacted angrily when provoked by others") and Proactive Aggression (e.g., "vandalized something for fun"). The Reactive Aggression subscale has 11 items of aggression in response to frustration, and the Proactive Aggression subscale has 12 items measuring instrumental aggression, responses that serve to achieve one's goals. There is also a Total Aggression score. A Spanish version is available (Andreu et al., 2009). Good internal consistency reliability and convergent validity were reported for a large ($n = 1,490$) sample of Spanish-speaking adolescents in a psychometric study of the Spanish version (Fernández et al., 2013).

Dimensions of Anger Reactions (DAR) (Forbes et al., 2014): Novaco's (1975) DAR-5 scale includes five items addressing anger frequency, intensity, duration, aggression, and interference with social functioning and scored on a 5-point Likert-type scale (1 = *none of the time*, 2 = *a little of the time*, 3 = *some of the time*, 4 = *most of the time*, and 5 = *all of the time*). The scale total is summative with the scale score ranging from 5 to 25. Higher scores indicate worse symptomatology. Modifications to the previous report of the DAR-5 include a specified time period, with items rated over the past 4 weeks and removal of frequency references from the items themselves. For example, a stem was included of "Thinking over the past 4 weeks, circle the number under the option that best describes the amount of time you felt that way," and item wording was changed to "I get angry at people and situations," with the word "often" removed. Previously, the DAR-5 was found to have high internal consistency (Cronbach's alpha of .88), and convergent validity was established, with strong correlations between the DAR and subscales of Trait Anger and Anger Out of the STAXI-CA.

Anger Strategies Scale (ASS) (Ronan et al., 1996; Ronan et al., 2004): This scale assesses 17 effective and 17 ineffective coping strategies that are used to deal with high-conflict situations. Effective coping strategies include accepting responsibility, compromising, describing the problem, paraphrasing/reflecting, and describing past positive behaviors. Ineffective coping strategies include denying responsibility, complaining, interrupting, criticizing, describing past negative behaviors, and name-calling. The ASS scale has not yet been evaluated with youth, and psychometric development has not been reported.

Anger-Related Reactions and Goals Inventory (ARGI) (Weber & Titzmann, 2003): This is a 56-item self-report inventory that combines the assessment of functional and dysfunctional anger-related reactions with the goals that people pursue in regulating interpersonal anger. There are seven Reaction subscales and seven Goals subscales. The four functional reactions selected are Problem-Oriented Behavior (providing feedback), Cognitive Restructuring (downplaying the incident's negative impact), Humor, and Distraction. The three dysfunctional reactions are Venting, Rumination, and Submission. The goals selected for the seven subscales are Enforcing Personal Standards, Enforcing Social Norms, Regulating Affect, Protecting Reputation, Weighing Costs, Avoiding Conflicts, and Taking Revenge. Each subscale consists of four items that are rated on a 4-point Likert-type scale (1 = *almost never* to 4 = *almost always*), with sum scores computed for each subscale. This scale has not yet been examined with adolescents, nor has there been sufficient psychometric research reported.

Beck Anger Inventory for Youth (BANI-Y) (Beck et al., 2001): BANI-Y is a 20-item self-report measure designed to assess anger in 7-year-olds to 14-year-olds. Children and adolescents rate, on a 4-point Likert-type scale ranging from 0 (*never*) to 3 (*always*), how frequently perceptions of mistreatment, negative thoughts about others, feelings of anger, and physiological arousal occur. The BANI-Y has relatively good psychometric properties for adolescents, with high internal consistency ($\alpha = .91-.92$) and moderately high test–retest reliability ($r = .76-.84$). The internal consistency for the measure in this study was also excellent for the sample in the present study ($\alpha = .92$) and for those participants who were 15 years and older ($\alpha = .93$).

Anger Rumination Scale (ARS) (Sukhodolsky et al., 2001): ARS measures the tendency to think about current anger-provoking situations and recall angry episodes from the past. It comprises 19 items, which load on four factors: Angry Afterthoughts (e.g., "After an argument is over, I keep fighting with this person in my imagination"), Angry Memories (e.g., "I ponder about the injustices that have been done to me"), Thoughts of Revenge (e.g., "I have long-living fantasies of revenge after the conflict is over"), and Understanding Causes (e.g., "I think about the reasons people treat me badly"). The items are rated on a 4-point Likert-type scale ranging from 1 = *almost never* to 4 = *almost always*. Possible scores on Angry Afterthoughts range from 6 to 42, with higher scores indicating more angry afterthoughts. The Thoughts of Revenge and the Understanding Causes subscales yield scores that range from 4 to 28, with higher scores indicating more thoughts of revenge and more time spent trying to understand causes. Possible scores on the Angry Memories subscale range from 5 to 35, with higher scores indicating more angry memories. All the items are phrased so that higher scores correspond to greater levels of anger rumination. Overall, the scale has been demonstrated to have adequate reliability and validity with a Cronbach's alpha of .93. Separate reliability coefficients for the four ARS subscales were Angry Afterthoughts, $r = .86$; Thoughts of Revenge, $r = .72$; Angry Memories, $r = .85$; and Understanding Causes, $r = .77$ (Maxwell et al., 2005; Sukhodolsky et al., 2001).

Adolescent Anger Rating Scale (AARS) (Burney & Kromrey, 2001): AARS was designed to (a) measure two distinct types of anger—instrumental and reactive—and (b) assist researchers and practitioners in identifying specific types of anger in adolescents 12 to 19 years old. Factor analysis on a revised 17-item inventory has three subscales: Instrumental Anger (7 items), Anger Control (5 items), and Reactive Anger (5 items). *Instrumental anger* is defined as anger patterns that are planned over a period of time and typically result in intensive violent and malicious attacks on people, places, or objects. *Reactive anger* is defined by responses that are immediately externalized (e.g., hitting) by the individual. Items are rated on a 4-point Likert-type scale of frequency from *hardly* to *very often*. Moderate to moderately high Cronbach's alphas and test–retest reliability coefficients indicated that scores from the AARS are internally consistent and stable when measuring anger subtypes. Discriminant validity evidence supported the AARS scores' ability to measure specific types of anger different from constructs of anger measured by the Multidimensional Anger Inventory (MAI).

Children's Emotion Management Scales (CEMS): Sadness (CSMS) and Anger (CAMS) (Zeman et al., 2001; Zeman et al., 2002): The Sadness and Anger Coping scales are indicators of emotion regulation. The Sadness subscale includes five items such as "I stay calm and don't let sad things get to me" and "I try to calmly deal with what is making me feel sad." One item ("When I am sad, I do something totally different until I calm down") was deleted to improve reliability (final Cronbach's alpha was .61 for adolescent report and .60 for parent report). The Anger subscale included four items such as "I can stop myself from losing my temper" and "I try to calmly deal with what is making me feel mad" (Cronbach's alpha was .74 for adolescent report, .79 for parent report). The wording of these items was modified for parents to report on their children. The scale ranges from 0 (*not true*) to 2 (*very true*). In moderation models, anger and sadness regulation were combined as composite scores based on parent and adolescent reports; correlations of $r = .36$, $p < .001$ were reported between parent and adolescent reports of anger regulation and $r = .25$, $p < .001$ for sadness regulation. In indirect-effects models, parent and adolescent reports of anger regulation were used as two indicators for the anger regulation latent construct, and parent and adolescent reports of sadness regulation were used as two indicators for the sadness regulation latent construct.

Children's Emotion Management Scales (Zeman et al., 2001) assess the self-report of children's Sadness (11 items) and Anger (12 items) management for children ages 8 to 12 years. Using a Likert-type scale of 1 (*hardly ever*), 2 (*sometimes*), or 3 (*often*), children respond to items that compose three subscales: (a) Inhibition (suppression of emotional expression; e.g., "I get sad inside, but I don't show it"), (b) Dysregulated Expression (children's culturally inappropriate emotional expression; e.g., "I say mean things to others when I am mad"), and (c) Emotion Regulation Coping (children's adaptive methods of emotion management; e.g., "When I am feeling sad, I do something totally different until I calm down"). Adequate psychometric properties have been demonstrated with coefficient alphas ranging from .60 to .77 and test–retest reliability ranging from .63 to .80 and evidence of convergent and discriminant validity with measures of emotion awareness, regulation, social functioning, and psychopathology (Zeman et al., 2001). In another study, internal consistency for sadness was Cronbach's alpha of .71, .57, and .66 for Inhibition, Emotion Regulation Coping, and Dysregulated Expression, respectively. For anger, internal consistency was Cronbach's alpha of .80, .72, and .69 for Inhibition, Emotion Regulation Coping, and Dysregulated Expression, respectively (Hurrell et al., 2015).

Assessment of Aggression

Peer Conflict Scale (PCS) (Marsee & Frick, 2007): This scale is a 40-item self-report assessing dimensions of aggression: 20 items for Reactive Overt and Reactive Relational Aggression ("When someone hurts me, I end up getting into a fight" or "If others make me mad, I tell their secrets") and 20 items assessing Proactive Aggression, both Proactive Overt ("I start fights to get what I want") and Proactive Relational ("I gossip about others to become popular"). Items are rated on a 4-point Likert-type scale (0 = *not at all true*, 1 = *somewhat true*, 2 = *very true*, and 3 = *definitely true*), and scores are calculated by summing the items to create the four subscales (range = 0–30). Research supports the distinction between the Reactive and Proactive scales as well as the Relational and Overt scales, in that they show unique associations with emotional and cognitive correlates (Marsee & Frick, 2007), narcissism and delinquency (Barry et al., 2007), and laboratory measures of aggression and psychophysiological correlates (Muñoz et al., 2008) in adolescent samples. Marsee et al. (2011) provided internal consistency estimates for 855 adolescents. The coefficient alphas for the combined sample were good: .82 for Proactive Overt, .80 for Proactive Relational, .89 for Reactive Overt, and .79 for Reactive Relational.

Revised Peer Experiences Questionnaire (RPEQ) (Prinstein et al., 2001): This scale is an 18-item self-report of aggression toward peers or victimization from peers on a 5-point Likert-type scale reflecting frequency. The aggressor version of the questionnaire has questions such as "I chased a teen like I was really trying to hurt him or her," whereas the victim version alters that question to read "A teen chased me like he or she was trying to hurt me." The Peer Experiences Questionnaire has been found to have good validity. Significant correlations between self-reported victimization and parent-reported victimization (rs between .36 and .39, $p < .001$) have been observed in two separate samples (Champion, 1997; Vernberg et al., 2000). Self-reported aggression and victimization on the Peer Experiences Questionnaire was significantly correlated with peer reports of the same constructs (rs between .34 and .40, $p < .001$). Test–retest reliability over a 6-month interval ranged from $r = .48$ to $r = .52$.

Inventory of Callous-Unemotional Traits (ICU) (Frick, 2003): This scale was developed as a 24-item self-report designed to assess callous and unemotional traits in youth. Each item (e.g., "I feel bad or guilty when I do something wrong," "I do not show my emotions to others") is rated on a 4-point Likert-type scale (0 = *not at all true*, 1 = *somewhat true*, 2 = *very true*, and 3 = *definitely true*). Scores are calculated by reverse-scoring the positively worded items and then summing the items to obtain a total score. This measure yields a total Callous-Unemotional traits score as well as three subscale scores: Callousness (a lack of empathy and remorse), Uncaring (an uncaring attitude about performance on tasks and others' feelings), and Unemotional (deficient emotional affect). Although designed as a self-report measure, research has shown the validity of using the measure with parent raters (Roose et al., 2010). The reliability and validity of the measure have been demonstrated in several studies (Ciucci et al., 2014; Essau et al., 2006; Kimonis et al., 2008; Roose et al., 2010). Internal consistency alpha coefficients ranged from .74 to .85. The ICU also showed significant positive associations with other measures of psychopathic traits. The ICU total score is associated with aggression, delinquency, and both psychophysiological and self-report indices of emotional reactivity in detained and incarcerated samples of youth.

How I Think Questionnaire (HIT-Q) (Barriga et al., 2001): This is a 54-item self-report questionnaire designed to measure self-serving cognitive distortions. Participants respond on a 6-point Likert-type scale ranging from 1 (*strongly agree*) to 6 (*strongly disagree*), with higher scores reflecting higher levels of cognitive distortions. The HIT-Q contains 39 items addressing self-serving cognitive distortions (Self-Centered, Blaming Others, Minimizing/Mislabeling, and Assuming the Worst) and one of the four antisocial behavioral categories of the *DSM-IV* (APA, 2000). These categories are opposition–defiance, physical aggression, lying, and stealing. Of the remaining 15 items, eight items control for anomalous responses that measure social desirability (e.g., "Sometimes I get bored"), and seven items act as positive fillers—that is, they camouflage items with a prosocial meaning (e.g., "When friends need you, you should be there for them"). The scale is currently available in Spanish and Dutch versions. Test–retest reliability was estimated at $r = .91$, and internal consistency coefficients, as measured by Cronbach's alpha, ranged from .92 to .96 across validation samples. The HIT-Q correlated with self- and parent-reported externalizing behavior in addition to measures of disruptive behavior, indicating good convergent validity. HIT-Q also successfully differentiated urban high school students from youth who were incarcerated, court referred for psychological evaluation, and hospitalized for disruptive behavior.

Parent Report

Peer Conflict Scale–Parent Report (PCS-PR) (Marsee et al., 2011): This scale is a 40-item questionnaire that parents fill out regarding their child's aggressive behavior with peers. The scale assesses Physical Proactive Aggression, Physical Reactive Aggression, Relational Proactive Aggression, and Relational Reactive Aggression. Each statement is rated on a 4-point Likert-type scale with scores ranging from 0 (*not at all*) to 3 (*definitely true*). Examples of items include "My child hurts others to win a game or contest" and "My child starts fights to get what he/she wants." This assessment differs from its predecessors in that it directly assesses harm to the victim, and its items are meant to gather more detail regarding the function of the aggressive behaviors. Internal consistency for the PCS scales in this study was satisfactory: Total Overt = 0.90, Reactive Overt = 0.87, Proactive Overt = 0.82, Total Relational = 0.87, Reactive Relational = 0.80, Proactive Relational = 0.76 (Marsee et al., 2014). Reactive and Proactive scales from the PCS were positively correlated with the youth's report of the number of violent delinquent acts ($r = 0.38$ and 0.55, respectively, both $p < 0.001$; Muñoz et al., 2008) providing support for validity.

Reactive–Proactive Aggression Questionnaire: Parent Version (RPA) (Dodge & Coie, 1987): The six items on the RPA provide a measure of reactive and proactive aggression. Parents use a 5-point Likert-type scale (1 = *never* to 5 = *almost always*) indicating how frequently each item applied to their child. Three items represent Reactive Aggression ("Overreacts angrily to accidents," "When teased, strikes back," and "Blames others in fights"), and three items represent Proactive Aggression ("Threatens or bullies others," "Gets others to gang up on a peer," and "Uses physical force to dominate others"). The construct validity of this version of the scale has been supported in prior studies (e.g., Vitaro et al., 2002).

Assessment of Emotion Regulation

Self-Report

Cognitive and Affective Mindfulness Scale–Revised (CAMS-R) (Feldman et al., 2007): On the basis of results of preliminary and confirmatory SEM models, 12 items were retained for a measure of mindful approaches to thoughts and feelings, which was called the Cognitive and Affective Mindfulness Scale–Revised (CAMS-R). This 12-item measure was shown to adequately sample the four domains of mindfulness (Attention, Present-Focus, Awareness, Acceptance/Non-Judgment). The items of CAMS-R are rated on a 4-point Likert-type scale from 1 (*rarely/not at all*) to 4 (*almost always*). Item 5 is reversely scored. The total score of the CAMS-R is obtained by computing the sum of all items. Higher scores on the scale suggest higher levels of mindfulness. The CAMS-R has been shown to possess acceptable levels of internal consistency ($\alpha = .81$, $n = 279$ [Greeson et al., 2011]; $\alpha = .77$, $n = 298$ [Feldman et al., 2007]). The overall CAMS-R, but not the subscales, demonstrated acceptable levels of internal consistency. The authors suggest the use of a single total mindfulness score rather than four subscale scores.

Emotion Regulation Questionnaire for Children and Adolescents (ERQ-CA) (Gullone & Taffe, 2011; MacDermott et al., 2010): This scale is a revised version of the adult Emotion Regulation Questionnaire (Gross & John, 2003) and includes 10 items that assess the emotion regulation strategies of cognitive reappraisal (six items) and expressive suppression (four items). Items are rated on a 7-point Likert-type response scale, and higher scores indicate greater use of the corresponding emotion regulation strategy. The version for children and adolescents was revised to include simplification of item wording (e.g., "I control my emotions by not expressing them" was reworded to "I control my feelings by not showing them") and reduction of the response length to 5 points (1 = *strongly disagree*, 2 = *disagree*, 3 = *half and half*, 4 = *agree*, and 5 = *strongly agree*). The example suppression item from the adult scale, "I keep my feelings to myself," was reworded for the child-and-adolescent scale to say, "When I am happy, I am careful not to show it." The example reappraisal item, "When I want to feel happier, I think about something different," was reworded to say, "When I want to feel happier about something, I change the way I'm thinking about it." The range of scores for each subscale is 6 to 30 (Reappraisal) and 4 to 20 (Suppression). The measure has demonstrated good internal consistency and adequate 4-week test–retest reliability (MacDermott et al., 2010). Confirmatory factor analysis reproduced the two factors proposed by Gross and John (2003). Validity has been demonstrated through correlations in the expected directions between the ER scales and a variety of measures such as temperament.

Difficulties in Emotion Regulation Scale (DERS) (Gratz & Roemer, 2004; Neuman et al., 2010): This scale is a 36-item questionnaire that assesses difficulties in regulating negative, aversive emotions. Participants indicate on a 5-point Likert-type scale (1 = *almost never* to 5 = *almost always*) how often each item applies to them (e.g., "I am attentive to my feelings" and "When I am upset, I start to feel very bad about myself"). Scores on four subscales (Non-Acceptance of Emotional Responses, Impulse Control Difficulties, Lack of Emotional Awareness, and Limited Access to ER Strategies) were reverse-coded and averaged to obtain an index of emotional engagement. These subscales reflect relationships with, and attitudes about, emotions and were selected because of their lack of redundancy with the other ER measures in the study. The DERS has demonstrated high internal consistency and convergent validity in both adult and adolescent samples (Gratz & Roemer, 2004; Weinberg & Klonsky, 2009).

Abbreviated Dysregulation Inventory (ADI) (Mezzich et al., 2001): This is a 30-item self-report measure designed to assess three different types of dysregulation in adolescents: emotional/affective, behavioral, and cognitive. The Behavioral Dysregulation subscale includes such items as "I get very fidgety after a few minutes if I am supposed to sit still." Participants rate each item on a 4-point Likert-type scale (0 = *never true* to 3 = *always true*), and scale items are averaged so that higher scores represent increased levels of dysregulation. Previous studies have reported adequate internal consistency coefficients for each of the subscales (Mezzich et al., 2001). In one sample of adolescents, the internal consistency of the Behavioral Dysregulation subscale was very good ($\alpha = .80$).

Emotion Expression Scale for Children (EESC): This is a 16-item child-report questionnaire for children 9 to 12 years old, originally adapted from the Toronto Alexithymia Scale (Bagby et al., 1986), which is a self-report measure of emotional expression difficulties in adults. The EESC contains two 8-item subscales measuring poor emotional awareness and reluctance to express emotions. Higher scores on these subscales indicate greater difficulties with emotional expression (Penza-Clyve & Zeman, 2002). Children are asked to rate statements using a Likert-type scale from 1 (*not at all true*) to 5 (*extremely true*). Scores range from 8 to 40 for each subscale, with higher scores reflecting more difficulties with awareness and expression of emotions. The EESC has demonstrated high internal consistency and moderate test–retest reliability in a community sample of children ages 9 to 12 (Penza-Clyve & Zeman, 2002) and has been utilized in previous studies of children diagnosed with anxiety disorders (Suveg et al., 2009; Trosper & May, 2011) as well as of adolescents diagnosed with eating disorders. The EESC has been used to measure vulnerabilities in emotional expression in community youth samples with elevated anxiety as well as clinically anxious children.

Affective Style Questionnaire (ASQ) (Hofmann & Kashdan, 2010): This is a 20-item measurement of individual differences in emotion regulation. The subscales are Concealing (referring to habitual attempts to conceal or suppress affect); Adjusting (a general ability to adjust, manage, or work with emotions as needed), which subscale consists of seven items that reflect the ability to balance and adjust to day-to-day emotional demands (e.g., "I can get out of a bad mood very quickly"); and Tolerating (an accepting and tolerant attitude toward emotion). The Concealing and Adjusting subscales consist of eight items that reflect the ability to manage the display of emotions (e.g., "I can hide my anger very well if I have to"), and the Adjusting participants indicated on a 5-point Likert-type scale (1 = *not true of me at all* to 5 = *extremely true of me*) how true emotion-related statements were of them. Both the Concealing and Adjusting subscales have demonstrated good internal consistency (Hofmann & Kashdan, 2010).

Emotion Regulation Skills Questionnaire (ERSQ) (Berking & Znoj, 2008): The ERSQ is a 27-item self-report measure that assesses application of emotion regulation skills during the previous week on a 5-point Likert-type scale (*not at all* to *almost always*). It contains nine scales that correspond to the nine emotion regulation skills previously discussed. Items are preceded by the stem "Last week" and are phrased (a) "I paid attention to my feelings," (b) "my physical sensations were a good indication of how I was feeling," (c) "I was clear about what emotions I was experiencing," (d) "I was aware of why I felt the way I felt," (e) "I was able to accept my negative feelings," (f) "I felt strong enough to tolerate even negative emotions," (g) "I supported myself in emotionally distressing situations," (h) "I could do what I intended to do despite my negative feelings," and (i) "I was able to influence my negative feelings." Results from validation studies (Berking & Znoj, 2008) indicate that both the total score and the subscales of the ERSQ have good internal consistencies (Cronbach's $\alpha = 0.90$ and 0.68–0.81, respectively) and adequate test–retest reliability ($\alpha = 0.75$ and 0.48–0.74, respectively). All scales have demonstrated convergent and discriminate validity, including strong positive correlations with constructs related to emotion regulation (Berking & Znoj, 2008). Sensitivity to change has been demonstrated in several samples of patients undergoing psychotherapeutic treatment (Berking & Znoj, 2008). Moreover, in two recent studies with 1,081 total participants, the ERSQ was shown to predict subsequent indicators of emotional adjustment over and above previous adjustment, whereas indicators of emotional adjustment did not predict subsequent ERSQ scores (Berking et al., 2008). These findings suggest that the skills assessed with the ERSQ do not merely represent a symptom of mental health problems.

Mindful Attention and Awareness Scale (MAAS) (Brown & Ryan, 2003): The MAAS measure includes fifteen 6-point Likert-rated items, focused on the most important characteristics of mindfulness—namely, an open and receptive awareness of and attention for what is happening here and now. The MAAS uses a participant rating scale from 1 (*almost always*) to 6 (*almost never*). Scoring involves calculating mean ratings across the 15 items, with higher scores indicating greater mindfulness. Brown et al. (2011) modified the scale for adolescent use by eliminating a single item. The MAAS is a reliable instrument that assesses a unique quality of awareness, predicting self-regulation and well-being. Psychometric adequacy was evaluated in a study of 595 adolescents, and high internal consistency, test–retest reliability, and concurrent and incremental validity estimates were reported. There are French and Spanish versions available.

Parent Report

Emotion Regulation Checklist (ERC) (Shields & Cicchetti, 1997): This is a 24-item measure of caregivers' perceptions of their youth's ability to regulate emotion. Items on the ERC assess the frequency with which youth exhibit a variety of positive and negative emotion regulation-related behaviors (e.g., "Can say when s/he is feeling sad, angry or mad, fearful or afraid," "Shows positive feelings in response to friendly or helpful gestures by adults") and are rated on a 4-point Likert-type scale (1 = *rarely/never* to 4 = *almost always*). The ERC contains two separate orthogonal factors: (a) Lability/Negativity, which reflects items assessing mood swings, angry reactivity, emotional intensity, and dysregulation of positive emotion; and (b) Emotion Regulation, which reflects processes central to the adaptive regulation of emotion, including equanimity, emotional understanding, and empathy (Shields & Cicchetti, 1997).

Emotion Expression Scale for Children: Parent Version (EESC-P) (Kerns et al., 2014): Based upon the EESC, items were adapted and reworded to reflect the parent as informant. Respondents rate the extent to which they agree with each of 16 items along a 5-point Likert-type scale (1 = *not at all true*, 3 = *somewhat true*, 5 = *extremely true*). The two subscales are Emotional Reluctance and Poor Awareness. Scores can range from 16 to 80, and higher scores indicate that the parent believes their child experiences greater difficulties with emotional expression. Split-half reliability estimates were high for both subscales, indicating very good internal consistency, and parent–child concordance was low-to-moderate within a subset of participants whose children completed the EESC (Kerns et al., 2014).

Assessment of Temperament

Self-Report

Revised Early Adolescent Temperament Questionnaire (EATQ-R) (Muris & Meesters, 2009): This 75-item scale measures reactive and regulative temperament factors for youth 9 to 15 years of age. It includes the following subscales: Activation Control, Activity Level, Affiliation, Attention, Fearfulness, Frustration, High-Intensity Pleasure, Inhibitory Control, Perceptual Sensitivity, Pleasure Sensitivity, and Shyness. There are also two behavioral scales for Aggression and Depression, and there are both parent and self-report child versions. Each item is rated on a 5-point Likert-type scale ranging from 1 = *almost never true* to 5 = *almost always true*. Temperament trait scores can be computed by summing ratings across relevant items (after recoding inversely formulated items). Test–retest correlations across an 8-week time frame for 101 youth indicated good reliability for all scales. Parent–child correlations for EATQ-R temperament scales (*n* = 390) varied between *r* = .33 (Affiliation, Frustration, and Perceptual Sensitivity) and *r* = .59 (Activity Level), suggesting that the parent–child agreement of various EATQ-R scales was low to moderate (Muris & Meesters, 2009).

Interpersonal Reactivity Index (IRI) (Davis, 1983): This 28-item self-report instrument was designed to measure cognitive and affective dispositions related to empathy. The four subscales (of seven items each) measuring Perspective-Taking (e.g., "I try to look at everybody's side of a disagreement before making a decision"), Empathic Concern (e.g., "I often have tender, concerned feelings for people less fortunate than me"), Fantasy (e.g., "I really get involved with the feelings of the characters in a novel"), and Personal Distress in Response to Stressful Situations (e.g., "Being in a tense emotional situation scares me") are included. Items were rated on a 5-point Likert-type scale (1 = *not true about me* to 5 = *extremely true about me*), and scale items were averaged so that higher scores represent increased levels of the attribute assessed. This measure has displayed acceptable internal consistency and evidence of predictive and convergent validity (Davis, 1983; Davis & Franzoi, 1991). Recently, a number of problems—including some uncertainty about its factor structure, low reliabilities, and poor readability of some items for people with limited literacy—have been identified. To address these issues, an abbreviated form of the index, the Brief IRI (B-IRI), was developed by Ingoglia et al. (2016). They demonstrated that the 16-item B-IRI has a clear and coherent factor structure, adequate internal consistency, measurement invariance across gender and age, and theoretically meaningful associations with a range of external criteria that support its construct validity. The B-IRI substantially preserves the psychometric properties of the long form and is recommended for use in all research settings (Ingoglia et al., 2016).

Revised Dimensions of Temperament Survey (DOTS-R) (Windle & Lerner, 1986): This 54-item self-report inventory is meant to measure temperament and assesses how people behave rather than how well they perform on tasks. It is suitable for youth ages 10 to 18. It includes 10 subscales: Activity Level–General (higher scores indicate higher energy levels), Activity Level–Sleep (higher scores indicate more motor activity during sleep), Approach–Withdrawal (higher scores indicate inclination toward new people and activities), Flexibility–Rigidity (higher scores indicate flexibility to environment changes), Mood Quality (higher scores indicate more positive affect), Rhythmicity–Sleep (higher scores indicate more regular sleep–wake cycles), Rhythmicity–Eating (higher scores indicate more regular eating habits), Rhythmicity–Daily Habits (higher scores indicate regular timing of diurnal activities), Distractibility (higher scores indicate better ability to concentrate), and Persistence (higher scores indicate tendency to continue certain activities for a longer period of time). Test–retest correlations for a sample of 179 late-adolescent subjects with an interval of 6 weeks between occasions of measurement ranged from $r = .62$ to $r = .79$ across the 10 subscales. Internal consistency indicates acceptable levels of reliability. The test–retest coefficients for the 10 scales and the second-order factors indicate moderate levels of stability of individual differences. Convergent correlations, reflecting inter-rater agreement between adolescents and their primary caregivers, are statistically significant ($p < .01$) of low-to-moderate magnitude. Gender groups differed significantly—$F(10, 935) = 8.38$, $p < .001$—in that boys reported higher levels of rhythmicity, or regularity of eating and sleeping habits, as well as higher levels of persistence and lower levels of distractibility; and girls reported higher levels of approach behavior, or sociability, and higher levels of positive mood quality (Windle, 1992).

Parent Report

Revised Early Adolescent Temperament Questionnaire (EATQ-PR) (Ellis & Rothbart, 2001): The EATQ-PR is a 62-item parent-report questionnaire measuring early adolescent temperament dimensions. Items are rated 1 to 5, ranging from *almost always untrue of your child* to *almost always true of your child*. EATQ-PR items are scored to generate scales for four higher order traits (Negative Affectivity, Affiliation, Surgency, and Effortful Control) and 10 lower order facet scales (Activation Control, Affiliation, Aggression, Attention, Depressive Mood, Fear, Frustration, High-Intensity Pleasure, Inhibitory Control, and Shyness). The internal reliability (Cronbach's alpha) of the EATQ-PR factors calculated in a Spanish sample ($n = 69$) were good (EC = .84, AF = .73, E/S = .42, NA = .63) for the parent-report questionnaire (Checa et al., 2008).

Section Two

Chapter 3

Preparation for TAME: Planning for Program Implementation

Introduction: Getting Ready to Start

Preparation and planning are necessary elements of effective therapy treatment groups. Before starting to use the TAME protocol, there are several factors to consider. The next section reviews those factors to consider before starting a TAME group, including (a) who is best suited for participating in TAME groups, (b) screening and assessment, (c) composition of groups, (d) outcomes planning, and (e) psychoeducation suggestions for individuals associated with TAME participants (teachers, parents, etc.)

What Is TAME?

TAME is a multicomponent program designed for use with early to late adolescents (ages 12–17). It consists of 11 sessions and one optional booster session for follow-up or maintenance purposes. The TAME program includes session-by-session instructions for the clinician, including role plays, homework assignments, in-session handouts and worksheets, and interactive teaching activities designed to engage the adolescent group and facilitate skill acquisition. Fidelity checklists are provided to allow group leaders to self-assess how much of the session content was covered. These checklists can be used for supervision purposes or as a self-monitoring technique for group leaders.

Who Is a Good Candidate for TAME Intervention?

As its full name implies, TAME was designed specifically for use with adolescents. The program is geared toward engaging and providing psychoeducation to individuals between the ages of 12 and 17. Examples, assignments, and activities in TAME draw from "typical" teenage struggles and difficulties including parent–child interactions, relational aggression, bullying, and conflicts related to social media. TAME may be appropriate for adolescent anger-related issues ranging from peer-interaction problems and school difficulties to more serious behavioral issues including conduct disorder, truancy, and criminal behaviors. The following clinical diagnoses may be appropriately served using the TAME treatment: conduct disorder, disruptive mood dysregulation disorder, impulse control and conduct disorders, oppositional defiant disorder, and intermittent explosive disorder.

Screening and Assessment

Prior to accepting clients for group intervention using TAME, appropriate screenings and assessments should be conducted. Screenings should focus on comorbid issues including intellectual or developmental disabilities, psychiatric conditions, and substance abuse problems. TAME was designed for typically developing adolescents and may not be appropriate for adolescents with intellectual or developmental disabilities. Appropriate modification to the program would be necessary in order to meet the specific needs of this population. Additionally, TAME may not be appropriate for adolescents with serious mental illness (e.g., psychotic disorders), serious depression, or suicidal behavior. Although anger may manifest as a symptom of some serious mental illnesses, specialized treatment focused specifically on those disorders may be more effective and ethically responsible. Also, TAME does not specifically address substance-abuse problems. Therefore, TAME may be combined with other treatments but should not be used solely in cases where substance abuse may be the primary area of concern.

When conducting an assessment of potential clients for TAME group intervention, the following methods should be considered:

1. A thorough clinical interview to gather information concerning the adolescent's particular anger management issues; a review of the referral, which usually includes concern on the part of staff that the particular youth does not know how to regulate their anger in appropriate and mature ways; and a review of several past incidents in which the youth lost their temper and perhaps suffered consequences such as detention or suspension, which can be discussed in an attempt to provide an initial sequential analysis or FBA of typical scenarios. We do recommend that the interview be done with a nonjudgmental attitude and that the youth be encouraged to provide their own accounts. Neutral terms such as "hassles" or "conflict" can be used to help the

interviewer understand what challenges the youth faces and what skill areas might need development.

2. Chapter 2 details all of the current paper-pencil measures that can be used to assess a youth's difficulties with anger management, aggressive behavior, and emotion regulation. There are particular measures that help examine anger provocation, anger responses, aggressive thinking, and attitudes toward anger management. Further, there is a description of paper-pencil measures that can be given to parents, teachers, and other staff members. Because the majority of these measures do not have large normative samples and therefore are not standardized, the scores cannot be used to determine whether or not the youth referred for anger management falls in a high-risk clinical range. However, the completion of paper-pencil measures by the adolescent and both parent and teacher can provide a baseline assessment before TAME is implemented. At the completion of the intervention program and also at follow-up dates, the same measures can be readministered to assess change in the youth and perhaps change in the outcomes of the TAME intervention for the whole group. We advise using at least two of the described measures, even though there has been research to indicate that self-report assessment methods with adolescents are far from reliable. Further, we suggest that at least one adult in the youth's life be asked to provide initial assessment data in the form of responses to an inventory that targets the behavior problems, even though there is often minimal agreement between the adolescents' and the adults' reports.

3. There are potentially many other sources of information/data that can be used to determine the outcomes of participation in a TAME program. In any education or clinical setting, there are programmatic data collected on a routine basis by others. These archival data sources are those that are routinely collected as a part of already existing programs and/or administrative policies and may easily be incorporated into any intervention effort. Baseline data is usually available for many weeks—even months and years—prior to an intervention, and data will continue to be collected following any treatment program. These typical school records may include absences, detentions, suspensions, demerits, expulsions, rule violations, class cuts, academic data (both local and statewide), grades in classes, homework completion, error rates, test scores, teacher evaluations, yearly reports, IEP data, nurses' notes, fines or other response cost measures from a behavior management system, and so on. Such data are easily collected by teachers as well as by treatment providers and, as such, are both time and cost efficient. Any source of

information that can be quantified can be charted across time for visual analysis of baseline stability and behavioral changes. For mental health personnel, we recommend keeping data on setting and keeping appointments, being on time, behavior during sessions (cooperation, compliance with tasks, verbal participation, eye contact, etc.), homework completion (i.e., self-monitoring or other task assignment), and contacts with family members and other professionals involved with the student. For some older students, there may also be community agencies involved with the target student and that might be able to provide data that is already being collected (once permission has been obtained). Police and probation departments, and other community organizations the student might be involved in (sports teams, scout clubs, etc.), might provide information about attendance and appropriate social behavior.

4. Finally, during this pre-intervention assessment phase, one should consider appropriate referrals and conjunctive treatments such as (a) individual therapy, (b) family therapy, (c) necessary social supports for family/caregivers (including social workers), and (d) psychiatric intervention (depression, ADHD, school problems, etc.).

Group Versus Individual Considerations When Using TAME

First, a decision must be made concerning whether to use individual or group treatment. Although there are no comparative data that indicate the superiority of one approach over the other with the aggressive-adolescent population, both individual and group TAME interventions have resulted in improved outcomes. Group interventions certainly have the advantage of multiple models and sources of feedback, increasing the probability of spontaneous and naturalistic provocations. This results in a greater opportunity for direct prompting and reinforcement for more appropriate responses to interpersonal provocations from peers. Admittedly, it is challenging to run a group of aggressive teens—especially in a context where they already know one another (e.g., from schools or residential facilities). This requires an effective leader who can use the already established peer relationships and their actual disagreements/conflicts for more in vivo anger management training. There is nothing quite like the "here and now" experience of de-escalating conflict and solving the issue with the skills taught within the program.

There are, however, some other considerations that might prioritize an individual approach to TAME. An individualized treatment plan may be indicated due to motivational, verbal/cognitive, or attention deficits of the youth referred for TAME. Adolescents who have interfering behavioral or impulse control issues such as self-abuse, drug involvement, or suicidal behaviors; who express concern over confidentiality of treatment; or who are extremely socially anxious and withdrawn would seem more appropriate for an individual approach. Within a particular setting, there is the possibility that bully–victim relationships exist and that these dynamics might dominate, thus precluding the participation of particular group members. Finally, because it may be that various subtypes of aggressive adolescents may respond differently to various components of the anger control program, individualized protocols may be most effective and efficient. TAME can serve as a resource for any mental health professional who might be working with a teen on multiple issues that seem related to anger management. What the research literature tells us is that emotion dysregulation characterizes many diagnostic categories and that most youth with emotional and/or behavioral difficulties will benefit from learning problem solving, mindfulness, and interpersonal effectiveness skills.

Consideration for Group Membership

When recruiting and assigning participants to a group intervention, several demographic variables can contribute to the effectiveness of the treatment. Although these variables cannot always be controlled in typical practice, clinicians are advised to be aware of them and customize the group intervention to best meet the unique constellation of group members. The first factor to consider is age: TAME is designed for an adolescent population. The period of adolescence results in a wide range of skills, knowledge, and maturity. Group members in early adolescence may benefit from being grouped with other younger adolescents with whom they can share examples and experiences. For example, a 13-year-old may not fully benefit from TAME if grouped with older adolescents (e.g., 17- and 18-year-olds). Group leaders should consider age and maturity when arranging group membership. An immature 16-year-old may be more appropriate in a TAME group composed of 13- and 14-year-olds as opposed to same-aged peers. Role plays and examples used during the course of treatment can and should be modified to match the ages and maturity levels of group participants.

Gender composition is another factor to consider when developing a TAME group. Research on gender differences regarding anger-related problems is mixed. Some findings suggest that boys exhibit higher levels of aggression, but when relational aggression is considered, the gender gap closes. Although the levels of youth anger may be similar, the expression of this anger may differ depending on gender. As a result, group leaders should customize examples and role plays to match the gender composition of the group (including more examples of relational aggression for an all-female TAME group). Group leaders should consider the pros and cons of single-sex versus mixed-gender groups. Single-sex groups may enhance the group's ability to focus on gender-specific issues related to anger; however, mixed-gender groups may help group leaders expand the scope of anger discussions and provide a full opportunity to practice these skills with both male and female teens. Developmentally, teens are extremely relationally focused, and attention to flirtation and intimate relationships is often a priority. This might be disruptive in a group process—or the anger management group might instead be the ideal context in which to practice emotion management in interpersonal conflicts.

In addition to age and gender, ethnic and racial composition of group members should be considered and used to individualize the experience of TAME groups. The stigma associated with psychological treatment in general may prevent members of some ethnic and racial groups from fully participating in anger management interventions. Group leaders should be aware of cultural factors that may serve as barriers to effective treatment. Cultural competence should also be considered when modifying examples, role plays, and homework assignments.

Aside from demographic factors, group leaders should also consider the relationship *between* group members when composing a TAME group. Groups implemented in school or residential settings are particularly likely to include group members that have preexisting relationships. This may be less of concern for groups run in clinical settings (outpatient clinics). For several reasons, group sessions may benefit from group members knowing each other: Role plays and examples given by group members may be more relevant and interesting to other group members, group members can reinforce and prompt skill use outside the group, active conflict between group members can be worked on in vivo during the group, the sense of group cohesion can be increased, and groups may be attended at higher rates when composed of familiar peers. However, groups with members who are already familiar to each other can potentially increase the risk of a confidentiality breach and may increase the level of distraction during group sessions. If group members have existing relationships outside the group, additional focus should be placed on group rules (e.g., confidentiality). Group leaders should specifically discuss the ways in which participating in TAME may and may not affect relationships among group members.

Outcomes Planning: Data Collection Methods

Planning ahead to guarantee support for the anger management intervention program that might be helpful to youth in various educational and clinical environments is always beneficial. The assessment methods described above for individual teens as anger management intervention begins should be administered at least at the beginning of a TAME intervention and then again at the end. This is known as *pre-to-post evaluation* and allows for an individualized assessment of treatment gains. A youth who has participated in the TAME program can be given this feedback to reinforce their efforts toward change and as evidence of actual change. This can be very empowering. These change scores can also be included in a year-end assessment of a youth's progress in a clinical setting or as part of a special education environment. Finally, it might be advantageous to include actual results from pre-to-post measurement to parents, teachers, and other caregivers. If there has been no pre-to-post change, these results should also be considered on an individual basis as well in order to determine readiness on the part of the teen and/or suitability of this type of intervention and need for additional/different services.

Outcomes data collection makes it possible to evaluate the impact of a TAME intervention using group aggregate data. If each member of the TAME group participates in the same pre-to-post assessment process, data can be summarized to indicate the overall effectiveness of the group intervention. In order to ensure that these data truly reflect the outcomes for the group, the same measures must be administered at the same times for both the pre- and the post-assessment. These data can help in obtaining administrative support for further programming and might help if program leaders are seeking funding for TAME interventions. Additionally, these data are usually more anonymous, as just group means are reported. This protects the confidentiality of the data and might increase the compliance with completing measures. If assessment tools are also given to parents and teachers at pre- and post-group interventions, this will help to determine the generalization of behavior change across environments. The ultimate goal would be for others to report that they have seen significant changes in the teen who received TAME at their school or other service environment.

Aside from formal assessment measures, Hassle Logs and archival data may also be used to assess outcomes. Hassle Logs require group participants to provide self-ratings of the intensity of anger and the perceived effectiveness in responding to daily "hassles" (i.e., anger-provoking situations). These ratings may be an additional source of data regarding the adolescent's subjective experience managing provocation. Depending on the setting in which TAME groups are conducted, archival data may be used to assess treatment progress. TAME groups conducted in residential or hospital settings may use data on restraints and critical incidents to evaluate treatment effectiveness. Information from school settings, including frequency of detentions and suspensions, may also be used for outcomes assessment.

Psychoeducation of Students, Teachers, Parents, and Other Caregivers

While the focus of the TAME program is to provide skills training and cognitive behavioral treatment to adolescents, treatment may be best enhanced by providing psychoeducation to caregivers and other influential adults. Group leaders should consider providing parents and other caregivers with basic psychoeducation about anger management and the rationale for this type of intervention prior to initiating group treatment with the adolescents. The period in which adolescent group participants are being recruited is an ideal opportunity to provide caregivers with an understanding of basic principles of anger management and the group therapy process. TAME groups that are conducted in school settings should include similar psychoeducation to teachers and school personnel. Failure to educate the caregivers and influential adults in the lives of these adolescents can result in intentional or unintentional treatment-interference behaviors. For example, caregivers may fail to prioritize TAME-group attendance over participation in extracurricular activities, resulting in numerous absences or instances of tardiness. This is disruptive to the therapeutic process of the adolescent and the group process. School administrations that rely on suspensions for disciplinary actions may unintentionally prevent students from receiving needed anger treatment. Thus, group leaders should ensure that prior to initiating treatment, school personnel are educated and supportive of the TAME program. In addition to psychoeducation about anger management prior to starting sessions, parents/caregivers may benefit from communication about it throughout the treatment process. Caregiver communication logs (see Appendix C) allow caregivers and the group leaders to share relevant information during the treatment process. Communication logs allow group leaders to share what was covered in each session and provide caregivers with specific tasks that can be worked on at home to reinforce concepts discussed in group. Ideally, these communication logs with caregivers will increase compliance with homework assignments as well.

Critical Treatment Elements

The three most critical treatment elements of the TAME protocol are Hassle Logs, in-session activities, and a focus on mindfulness and problem solving.

Hassle Logs

Although it is always best to collect some direct observation ratings as well as some pre-to-post questionnaire data from those who are interacting with the youth (parents, teachers, staff), assessment of the experience of anger and the hypothesized precursors of aggressive behavior requires a more subjective data collection method. The Hassle Log, a daily self-monitoring form, was created in order to quantify the variables associated with both the antecedent and consequent conditions surrounding aggression from the perspective of the adolescent. A number of categories requiring only a simple check off are included, as adolescent clients sometimes have only limited focus to complete anything lengthier. Always mindful of not giving them anything to carry around that might signal that they are in anger management treatment, the simple four-entry Hassle Log folds and fits neatly into a back pocket of their jeans (see Appendix A: Worksheet 1b).

Although there are limited expectations for the accuracy, reliability, or validity of these self-monitoring data, the Hassle Log has become an extremely valuable clinical and educational tool and is always cited as a foundational component of TAME. Research evaluations of the anger management program in residential and educational settings have included this Hassle Log, although it served less often as a source of reliable outcome data and more as a training method. It further can serve these other clinical objectives:

- **Teaching tool**: The Hassle Log serves as a way to determine individual sequences of triggers, setting events, responses, and self-evaluation.

- **Scripts for role plays**: The recording of situational events in the Hassle Log by the adolescents themselves provides realistic scenarios for enactments during the sessions.

- **Alternative response to triggers**: Often youth turn to these diary-type checklists instead of responding to the triggering event.

- **Teaching about self-observation and reflection**: The items ask the adolescent to stop and reflect as they read and check off items.

- **Compliance probe early in therapy**: Each TAME session concludes with a relevant homework exercise to ensure that skills learned will be practiced and might generalize to the home environment. The assignment of the Hassle Log in the first session allows the group leader to assess the general compliance toward these types of homework assignments. Thus, noncompliance can be addressed right away.

- **Portable reminder**: The Hassle Log can function as a generalization strategy in that it brings the treatment into other contexts and environments.

- **Prompter of self-reinforcement for alternative responses to provocation**: In fact, completing a Hassle Log instead of responding to the perceived provocation might work out far better in terms of outcomes for the adolescent.

- **Visual motor exercise**: This is an advantage in contrast to the auditory memory prompts of most instructions. Most of the TAME content is delivered via discussion and role-play, with some worksheets to reinforce key concepts. The Hassle Log is a visual motor task that will assist some learners in retaining the information more effectively.

The categories used on the self-monitoring form can be changed to adapt to either the client population or the environment for flexibility of format. Inconsistencies between perceived events and self-evaluation of responses and self-rating of affect can be examined and used to illustrate the components of an interactional sequence. This is especially useful when working individually with a teen.

Since its inception, the Hassle Log has undergone multiple transformations for youth and adult clients in treatment for problems with anger and aggression. A low-cost aspect of any intervention program, the Hassle Log serves many purposes in a user-friendly fashion. Although any data collected via self-monitoring is subject to inaccuracies and biases, these data can still be collected and graphed, thus providing a visual-reinforcement process for the clients. After all of these years, the Hassle Log continues to be an invaluable tool for TAME trainers and clients.

In-Session Activities

These include role plays, prompted discussions, and games that allow group members to practice anger management strategies and interventions. Anger management coping skills can be difficult for youth to implement in calm situations and impossible to use effectively in real-life scenarios without practice. During role plays, group members have an opportunity to attempt implementation of specific strategies and get feedback about their performance from peers and group leaders. This feedback may help to increase their confidence and willingness to attempt these strategies outside of the group. Group activities also serve to build rapport among group members and leaders. Some youth may learn from modeling, while others learn from doing. Active participation in the group discussion can be enhanced by role plays and games that help include participation of all group members.

Mindfulness and Problem Solving Focus

Mindfulness focuses on being present and nonjudgmental. Mindfulness activities are presented at the beginning of the group in order to orient the group's attention and focus. By developing mindfulness skills, group members are more likely to be able to implement other anger management coping skills when provoked. Group members may understand the strategies, but without the ability to delay responding and remain present-focused, skills may not be effectively implemented. Combining mindfulness and problem solving skills in one treatment protocol increases the likelihood that youth will be able to transfer skills learned in group to real-life situations.

Case Examples From the Initial Implementation of TAME

Case 1: Overhead Announcements

TAME was originally piloted in a middle school setting during the after-school program (see Chapter 6). Although this initially seemed like a reasonable time to conduct the groups, several factors proved otherwise. Using the after-school time period appealed to the group leaders because it meant that students involved in the TAME groups would not miss out on instructional time in the classroom and would easily be able to attend sessions immediately after school ended. This minimized the likelihood that sessions would be missed due to transportation issues or scheduling conflicts as might be expected in a clinic setting. However, TAME groups were difficult to run during this time period due to several distractions, the most obvious of which were the frequent overhead announcements. Announcements were made over the school's PA system at a rate of nearly three to five per hour. This meant frequent and sustained distractions during the group sessions, as the announcements were so loud that it was nearly impossible to continue a discussion while they occurred. Group members found it difficult to remain focused, and group leaders strained to get through all of the content during the 50-minute sessions. Although this example may be specific to the school environment in which the TAME program was initially studied, it highlights the importance of experiencing the environment in which group sessions are expected to take place before scheduling the group. Group leaders should examine the setting during the scheduling time period to ensure a reasonable level of privacy and minimal environmental distractions. This is especially important given the tendency of adolescents with anger-related issues to be easily distracted and impulsive.

Case 2: CT and Detention

CT was a 13-year-old enrolled in the TAME program at his middle school. He was referred for TAME groups because he engaged in several problematic behaviors that resulted in frequent school disciplinary actions. These included fighting with peers, cursing at his teachers, frequent absences from and lateness to school, and general noncompliance and oppositional behavior in the classroom. CT reported feeling angry much of the time and being unable to control his behaviors during these periods. He was an ideal candidate for the TAME program. However, he often missed group sessions due to having to serve detention or suspension. School officials who agreed to implement TAME groups in the school were simultaneously making it difficult, because of their unwillingness to modify school policies regarding detention and suspension, for students like CT to attend those sessions. This case highlights the importance of working with all relevant individuals affiliated with potential TAME group members prior to establishing group sessions. In situations in which TAME is used in or as part of a school setting, school administrators need to provide more than just approval to run TAME in the school—they must be involved in actively supporting the program. One way in which they can do this is to ensure that school policies such as detention and suspension are modified/adjusted to allow group members to fully participate in the TAME program. It should be expected that those who might benefit from TAME are likely to continue engaging in anger-related behaviors until they are able to apply the coping skills and cognitive behavioral strategies discussed in group. Given this expectation, some accommodations to existing school policies may be necessary to ensure maximal group participation.

Case 3: MK and the Angry Mother

MK was a 14-year-old who participated in TAME at her middle school. She initially was reluctant to participate in group discussions and denied having problems with anger. As group sessions progressed, she began offering examples of anger-related interactions with her mother; she described her mother as angry and out of control. Although she was able to acknowledge situational stressors that contributed to her mother's anger (including being a young mother working two jobs while trying to care for her children), MK often found it difficult to control her anger in response to her mother's sometimes-reasonable requests. MK more easily identified the consequences of uncontrolled anger in her mother (e.g., relationship issues and frequent fights with her child) than she did in herself (e.g., frequent school disciplinary action). However, becoming more aware of how angry her mother was allowed MK to become more aware of her own anger over time. While discussing assertive communication skills, MK reported that she was aware for the first time that her problems managing her anger were related to the fact that her mother served as a poor role model for how to manage strong emotions. She stated: "I act like she does, but because it is what I saw every day of my life." This became a turning point in MK's treatment, and she began to speak more openly and participate more fully in future group sessions. The intergenerational transmission of anger management is highlighted in this case example: MK modeled her own responses after her mother and as a result was less aware of other ways of being and of her own problems with anger. It was not as though she did not have other models of how to manage anger (e.g., teachers); however, her similarities to her mother made it such that she more closely resembled her mother in both attitude and behaviors. She reported in later sessions that what she had learned most from the group was that she had previously believed that the difference between her and others who did not engage in anger-related behaviors was something fundamental and unchangeable (e.g., "They just aren't bothered by the same things"). By the end of the group, she realized that anger was universal and appropriate and that she had a choice in how she responded and after whom she modeled herself. MK's case illustrates the possibility that co-occurring parenting groups or anger management for parents may be beneficial for adolescents. Although parenting groups are often associated with younger children, perhaps co-occurring parenting groups would benefit parents of teens by building coping skills and providing training on how to manage their own emotions and model appropriate communication. Teens may be better able to apply skills learned in TAME groups if their parents are provided with some of this information as well. Other therapeutic interventions, such as dialectical behavior training, have found parent training to be a necessary treatment intervention with impulsive teenagers (Miller et al., 2002).

Case 4: TG and the Sibling Issues

TG was a 13-year-old middle school student. She reported difficulties managing her anger toward her younger siblings (ages 9 and 10). TG was often responsible for supervising her siblings after school. She found it difficult to control their behavior and responded punitively and out of anger. TG reported that she felt "stuck" because she had a poor relationship with her siblings and was often "in trouble" for aggression toward them. However, when she allowed them to break rules and gave up trying to manage their behavior after school, she would also get in trouble with her mother. This experience added to her anger and made it difficult for her to manage feelings of resentment toward her siblings and to control her desire to retaliate against them. TG often spoke of the way in which it felt good to aggress toward her siblings and "release" the anger. It is not uncommon for anger management clients to endorse catharsis as a reason for engaging in aggression. Although research has demonstrated the opposite effect, many continue to believe that catharsis is effective in reducing feelings of anger. Rather than learning to inhibit this desire to release physical energy or channel it into a more controlled form of aggression (e.g., hitting a pillow), TG and others like her may benefit from recognizing other ways to physically release tension in their bodies (e.g., exercise or relaxation activities) and experiencing compassion for oneself and others. In TG's case, the responsibility of supervising younger siblings with behavioral problems may be outside the bounds of what any 13-year-old might be expected to accomplish, and allowing space for self-compassion may aid in managing some of her anger.

Anger toward the self and others is commonly experienced within this population, but feelings of compassion may need to be cultivated in order to provide greater balance of emotional experiences. For this reason, a self-compassion mindfulness exercise was added to the TAME program in order to help group members develop this skill. Because self-compassion mindfulness activities are among the most difficult, even for adults, it is recommended that this exercise be completed after group members have practiced several other mindfulness exercises.

Chapter 4

TAME Session-by-Session Protocol

This TAME protocol was modified from the original version published by Feindler and Gerber (2008).

Session 1: Group Orientation

    A) Introductions

    B) Introduce Emotions

    C) Introduce the Hassle Log

    D) Summary and Homework

Session 2: Self-Assessment of Anger and the ABCs of Behavior

    A) Collect and Review Hassle Logs and Homework Assignments

    B) Recap Previous Session

    C) Introduce Self-Assessment of Anger and the Concept of ABCs

    D) Exercises

    E) Summary and Homework

Session 3: Refuting Aggressive Beliefs

    A) Collect and Review Hassle Logs and Homework Assignments

    B) Recap Previous Session

    C) Mindfulness Activity

    D) Introduce Interpretation of Events

    E) Refuting Aggressive Beliefs

F) Exercise

G) Summary and Homework

Session 4: Being Mindful and Ending Rumination

A) Collect and Review Hassle Logs and Homework Assignments

B) Recap Previous Session

C) Mindfulness Activity

D) Introduce Mindfulness

E) Introduce the ABCs of Mindfulness

F) Explain What Mindfulness Is Not

G) Introduce Rumination

H) Exercises

I) Contrast Rumination and Reappraisal

J) Summary and Homework

Session 5: Assertiveness Techniques

A) Collect and Review Hassle Logs and Homework Assignments

B) Recap Previous Session

C) Mindfulness Activity

D) Introduce Objectives Effectiveness

E) Introduce Skills to Enhance Objectives Effectiveness

F) Exercise

G) Summary and Homework

Session 6: Relationship-Building Techniques

A) Collect and Review Hassle Logs and Homework Assignments

B) Recap Previous Session

C) Mindfulness Activity

D) Introduce Relationship Effectiveness

E) Relationship Effectiveness Skills: GIVE

F) Exercise

G) Summary and Homework

Session 7: Self-Instruction Training

A) Collect and Review Hassle Logs and Homework Assignments

B) Recap Previous Session

C) Mindfulness Activity

D) Introduce Self-Instruction Training

E) Application of Reminders Procedure: Overt and Covert Reminders

F) Exercises

G) Summary and Homework

Session 8: Thinking Ahead

A) Collect and Review Hassle Logs and Homework Assignments

B) Recap Previous Session

C) Mindfulness Activity

D) Introduce Thinking Ahead Procedure

E) Exercises

F) Summary and Homework

Session 9: Problem Solving Training

A) Collect and Review Hassle Logs and Homework Assignments

B) Recap Previous Session

C) Mindfulness Activity

D) Introduce Problem Solving Training

E) Exercises

F) Summary and Homework

Session 10: Bullying Prevention—Specific Problem Solving Techniques

A) Collect and Review Hassle Logs and Homework Assignments

B) Recap Previous Session

C) Practice Mindfulness Activity

D) Introduce Bullying Prevention and Relational Aggression

E) Distinguish Between Good Teasing and Bad Teasing

F) Exercise

G) Talking It Out

H) Apologizing

I) The Power of Words: Verbal Aggression

J) Introduce Self-Respect Effectiveness

K) Summary and Homework

Session 11: Program Review

A) Collect and Review Hassle Logs and Homework Assignments

B) Mindfulness Activity

C) Program Review

D) Discuss Situational and Personal Elements

E) Closing Remarks

F) Administer Posttest Questionnaires/Assessments (If Applicable)

Session 12: Follow-Up/Booster Session

A) Collect and Review Hassle Logs and Homework Assignments

B) Mindfulness Activity

C) Program Review

D) Closing Remarks

E) Administer Posttest Questionnaires/Assessments (If Applicable)

Session 1: Group Orientation

A. Introductions

1. Introduce coleaders, and have each group member introduce themself.

2. Discuss confidentiality and its limits.

3. Introduce the rationale of the program:

   a. To teach new skills that will enable the students to control their anger in provocative situations and decrease both overt and covert aggression as a response to anger.

   b. To increase the students' personal power by learning the skills necessary to communicate their needs and desires effectively.

4. Review rules of the program:

   a. Describe role plays, and introduce the need for participation.

   b. Describe mindfulness activities and the need for participation.

   c. Discuss participation in group discussions.

   d. If applicable, discuss use of points system, wherein a special prize is awarded to the persons with the highest point totals for appropriate behaviors during group meetings.

5. Practice simple mindfulness exercise (e.g., mindful breathing; see Appendix B).

B. Introduce Emotions

1. Explain basic information about the nature of emotions and moods.

2. Discuss how every culture gives names to emotions and that when people are able to describe and name an emotion, they understand it better and are better able to manage it.

3. Explain the steps in naming emotions:

   a. Recognize when you are feeling an emotion.

   b. Describe the emotion by considering

      » the provoking stimulus or event

      » the interpretation of the event (i.e., thoughts and beliefs)

      » physiological sensations

      » body language (e.g., face and posture)

      » verbal communication of the emotion

      » actions or behaviors taken in response to the emotion

4. Introduce the emotion of anger as the main focus of the group. Generate a discussion of how anger might be defined. Talk about variations in frequency and intensity.

5. Suggested exercises:

   a. Have students think about angry situations and try to describe what happens. Write on the board the physical and other cues students notice when they get angry.

   b. Have students name different intensities or variations of anger (e.g., hatred, frustration) and place them on a thermometer continuum from "warm" to "boiling."

   c. Introduce the brief relaxation technique Take Three: Taking three slow, deep breaths can help students maintain a controlled response to anger provocations. Give students examples of athletes (e.g., figure skaters, gymnasts, baseball players) who visibly use a few deep breaths before attempting some event. Remind students about their physiological cues: for example, muscle tension in the neck, lower back, or shoulders; fist clenching; cursing; gritting of the teeth; even heart palpitations. Explain that deep breathing will function to reduce physiological tension, refocus attention away from external provoking stimuli to the student's internal control, and provide a time delay before making a choice of how to respond.

   d. Have the students think about a situation in which they were very angry. They may need to be prompted with questions such as "Think, for a moment, of the last time someone really got you steamed" or "Can you remember the last time you were in a situation where you wanted to hit someone who was really pushing your buttons?" Have students enumerate what physiological and other cues they noticed. Write these cues on the board.

   e. Model for the students how, when they first notice that they are beginning to get angry, they should stop and remind themselves to relax and take one or two deep breaths.

   f. Have the students provoke each other. For example, one student might say to another, "Just get out of my face!" Ask them to say, "Relax" aloud and take the deep breaths. Role plays allow the group leaders to determine if the students understand this procedure and to provide opportunities for giving feedback.

g. Have the students practice diaphragmatic breathing: Tell them to imagine that they each have a balloon in their stomach and they have to blow it up without moving any other part of their body. Check to make sure they are not lifting and tensing their shoulders.

C. Introduce the Hassle Log

1. Run through an example of a hypothetical conflict with students to demonstrate how to fill out the Hassle Log.

2. Give the rationale for using a Hassle Log: It is a self-monitoring device that will provide each student with an accurate picture of how they handled conflict situations during the week. It is a device for students to learn what sets them off. It provides an opportunity to report situations that were different and that were handled well. Finally, it provides scripts for in-session role play.

D. Summary and Homework

1. Review mechanics of completing Hassle Logs.

2. Homework: Ask students to fill in their Hassle Logs after a conflict situation and attempting the Deep Breathing technique.

Session 2: Self-Assessment of Anger and the ABCs of Behavior

A. Collect and Review Hassle Logs and Homework Assignments

Review the importance of completing homework assignments (if any group members did not complete the assignment).

B. Recap Previous Session

Always review what was covered in the preceding session, and field any questions about skill implementation. For this session, review the brief relaxation techniques and ask students if they had any difficulty implementing this strategy in the past week. For example, the relaxation technique may not have been effective if the student continued to focus their attention on the provocative stimuli instead of on the deep breaths they were taking. Conduct brief mindfulness activity (see Appendix B) to orient the group's attention and focus.

C. Introduce Self-Assessment of Anger and the Concept of ABCs

These ABCs are *antecedents*, *behavior*, and *consequences*. Refer to the ABCs Worksheet (see Appendix A: Worksheet 7) so the students can visualize what is discussed.

1. Provoking stimulus: Start with "What gets you angry?" Discuss situational variables and setting events in terms of what is going on in the environment (overt activating events) and physiological states of fatigue, hunger, and so on (covert activating events).

2. Introduce the idea of *triggers* (anger-provoking activating events): In this discussion, focus on the beginning of the anger/aggression sequence.

   a. *Direct triggers:* These are direct aversive provocations by another person, which may be verbal (being told what to do) or nonverbal (a kick, push, obscene gesture, etc.).

   b. *Indirect triggers:* These aversive stimuli include the misperception or misattribution of events such as feeling blamed or feeling like someone is disapproving. Most of these events involve a faulty appraisal of what is going on, such as "He put me on restriction because he doesn't like me." Help students to identify different ways of interpreting provoking incidents.

3. Actual behavior/reaction: Ask "How do you know when you are angry?" Focus on the cognitive or physiological covert (inside) or overt (outside) cues that occur:

   a. Negative statements to self (e.g., "I'm an idiot" or, directed at others, "I want to kick them in the face").

     b. Physiological cues (e.g., muscle tension, rigid posture, angry stare, butterflies in stomach, tense facial muscles).

  4. Consequences: Inquire, "What happened to you as a result of not controlling your anger? Did you get in trouble?" There may also be positive consequences of temper loss, in that the individual may feel personal satisfaction or achieve some desired goal or object.

D. Exercises

  1. The Trigger Finger: Break students into two teams of equal number. Ask them to see which team can come up with the longer list of activating events or triggers that typically result in angry reactions. Each team has five minutes. Remind students that they can review their completed Hassle Logs for ideas.

  2. Model how direct triggers and indirect triggers (misattributions or misperceptions) can heighten a conflict. Then have students provoke each other. The student being provoked should relate the cognitive self-statements they generated in response to each provocative activating event.

  3. Going to the Head: Form two teams. Team A states a physiological cue, and Team B must identify a verbal overt (outside) or cognitive covert (inside) cue. If both teams give plausible cues, then a member of Team B must come up with a cognitive cue this time, and a member of Team A with a physiological cue. If one team member cannot respond, the other team has the chance to steal a point by coming up with a cue. For example, a member of Team A states that a physiological cue is "getting hot," and a member of Team B says a cognitive cue is "I'm going to kill him." These are both correct answers. Now a member from Team A must state a cognitive cue such as "She had better not take another step toward me," and a member from Team B must state a physiological cue such as "heart palpitations." Again, both teams are correct. Team A continues by stating a physiological cue, and Team B offers a cognitive cue. This time, however, Team A *incorrectly* identifies a physiological cue (such as "I'm going to smash him"), so Team B has a chance to steal a point. Team B does this by stating a correct cognitive cue (because Team A was wrong) and stating the physiological cue (which is what Team A was supposed to identify).

  4. Practice identifying the ABCs from role plays:

     a. Group leaders should role-play a provocative event (e.g., thinking that a peer or adult is lying with regard to something promised to them).

Demonstrate the identification of activating events, behaviors, and consequences.

b. Ask two group members to role-play a provocative event of their Hassle Logs. Have the actors and other members from the group identify activating events, behaviors, and consequences.

E. Summary and Homework

1. Review ABCs

2. Homework: Hand out additional ABCs worksheet, and assign the analyses of two incidents before the next session. Also, remind students to complete Hassle Logs (to be used for role play scripts).

Session 3: Refuting Aggressive Beliefs

A. **Collect and Review Hassle Logs and Homework Assignments**

B. **Recap Previous Session**

C. **Conduct Brief Mindfulness Activity to Orient the Group's Attention and Focus**

D. **Introduce Interpretation of Events**

Explain that most events do not automatically cause emotions. Instead, the emotion is caused by the person's *interpretation of the event* or how the person thinks about the event.

> ➤ Scenario for discussion (read aloud): Maria doesn't like Susan or Jenny. Susan gets very angry with Maria for not liking her, but Jenny just gets afraid. Why would they have two different emotions based on the same fact (that Maria doesn't like them)? Susan gets mad because she thinks about how much she has done for Maria. She believes Maria should appreciate it and like her. Meanwhile, Jenny feels frightened because she thinks that if Maria doesn't like her after all she has done for Maria, maybe *no one* will like her.

E. **Refuting Aggressive Beliefs**

1. Explain that sometimes we have beliefs about why people act in certain ways toward us. These beliefs lead to thoughts that another person is acting aggressively or nonaggressively.

2. Explain that there are both aggressive and nonaggressive ways to interpret situations. For example, a nonaggressive belief would be "If someone looks at me differently or acts differently toward me, maybe they are having a bad day."

3. Explain that interpreting situations in nonaggressive ways will help control anger responses.

F. **Exercise: All the Reasons Why**

1. Brainstorm and list all the attributions the group makes about why people act in certain ways or do certain things. For example, ask the group to write down reasons someone might have passed them in the hall and said some derogatory statement (e.g., "Bitch!") as they passed by. The students will probably generate a list of aggressive beliefs regarding what happened, such as "She did it on purpose," "She wants to start something with me," and so on.

2. Brainstorm and list all the alternative nonaggressive explanations for the examples in Part 1 (e.g., "She wasn't talking about me" or "She was having a bad day"). Generate alternative and nonaggressive attributions.

3. Have the group discuss whether the nonaggressive interpretations are or are not plausible interpretations. Then discuss how adopting a nonaggressive interpretation might change how you feel about the situation.

G. Summary and Homework

1. Review differences between aggressive and nonaggressive beliefs or interpretations of situations.

2. Hand out additional Hassle Logs for completion during the week.

Session 4: Being Mindful and Ending Rumination

A. **Collect and Review Hassle Logs and Homework Assignments**

B. **Recap Previous Session**

C. **Practice Ice Cube Mindfulness Activity to Orient the Group's Attention and Focus**

Group leaders should provide a few ice cubes for the group members to look at and feel during this activity. The group leaders should initiate the considerations: for example, by saying, "Take a look at these ice cubes. Notice the different features when water is in its frozen form. How does it look and feel?" ("When frozen, it is hard, cold, and painful to hold onto; you can't see through it; it is heavy; you can carry it with you.") The considerations should then be directed to a follow-up, such as "How is it different when it melts into a puddle?" ("It is smooth and easily runs through your fingers, it is light and silky against your skin, it is not as painful to hold, and you can see through it.")

D. **Introduce Mindfulness**

1. Explain that *mindfulness* is a way of paying attention and being more aware of what is happening in the present moment. It will not eliminate the stressors in life, but it can help you respond more calmly. Being mindful in your life means that you are better able to recognize your impulses and respond differently when you want to. Practicing mindfulness allows you be to more present in your life.

2. Explain that the brief activities that start each group are examples of how we can practice mindfulness. Mindfulness is a skill that needs to be exercised, and there are many ways to do it. Let the students know that in each group, they will practice a new activity in order to introduce them to all the ways in which they can exercise this skill.

E. **Introduce the ABCs of Mindfulness**

1. A is for **Awareness**: This means being more conscious of what you are thinking, doing, or feeling in the moment.

2. B is for just **Being**: To be mindful is to notice your experience without judging it or avoiding it. It means you can just sit with the feeling, sensation, and thought.

3. C is for **Choices**: When you are more aware of your thoughts, feelings, and actions, you have the power to make choices about how you want to

respond or not respond. For example, if you find yourself thinking "I'm smelling someone barbecuing," you can notice the thought and decide to act on it (by finding food) or not (just thinking to yourself "That smells good").

F. Explain What Mindfulness Is Not

Acting before thinking: "You know that feeling you get when you walk into a room to get something and then you can't remember why you even came in the room to begin with? It happens to everybody. This is what happens when you move about our world being mindless. Being more mindful will help with your ability to stay focused, make better choices, and be aware of your feelings without letting them control you."

G. Introduce the Idea of Rumination

Ruminating is thinking over and over about a certain emotional experience. We know that doing this intensifies the emotion rather than helping us positively deal with the emotion.

H. Exercises

1. Discuss this scenario: Emily and Joe are standing on the corner, waiting for the bus to arrive. Nervous about her upcoming test, Emily waits impatiently and mentally rehearses everything she can remember about the topic. Joe is to have the same test this morning, and he keeps checking his phone for the time. The bus finally arrives, but it will get them to school late. Emily ruminates during the bus ride and gets angrier by the minute, thinking over and over about all the things that are unfair: she has to take a bus to school, the bus is late, the driver doesn't care that she has to be somewhere, and so on. She is annoyed that, because of the lateness, she won't have enough time to review her notes before the test; she also worries that she will run out of time. Joe, however, reminds himself that it is only a test; he thinks about what he will tell the teacher when he arrives to class. He imagines that the teacher will be understanding and that everything will work out. When they arrive at school, both Emily and Joe rush to class. When the teacher asks why they are late, Emily can't control her response: She yells, "The freaking bus was late again!" The teacher quickly interrupts and pulls her to the side. Emily ends up getting in trouble and can't focus for much of the test. Now ask the students, "How you do you think things go with Joe?"

2. Remind the group of the Ice Cube mindfulness activity at the beginning of the session. Ask, "How is an ice cube like anger?" Group leaders

can discuss how time helps to reduce the strength of emotions (such as anger) and provide greater clarity regarding those emotions. Ask, "What is refreezing similar to?" Group leaders can then discuss rumination and its potential pitfalls.

I. **Contrast Rumination and Reappraisal**

1. Ask the group to give examples of things they have ruminated about. Discuss the urge to continue ruminating versus letting it go. Discuss what group members have done to attempt to stop rumination behavior in the past.

2. Often, it is not enough to just think of something different; instead, it is most helpful to *reappraise* the situation. This means finding another way to think about that event. For example: A friend agrees to do you a favor; you are really counting on this person, and they end up letting you down.

   a. *Rumination*: "I knew I shouldn't have trusted anyone—they only let me down! If they were a good friend, they would never have done that to me!"

   b. *Reappraisal*: "Everyone messes up. I myself have forgotten to do important things in the past, and I felt horrible about it. I bet my friend is feeling pretty bad about letting me down, too—or maybe they really didn't even understand how upset it would make me feel."

   c. *Practicing mindfulness* can help. Discuss with students how, by being more aware of their thoughts, feelings, and actions, they can catch themselves ruminating and change their thinking. Reappraisals can help de-escalate intense emotions and prevent them from getting angrier.

   d. "But what if I *can't* stop thinking about it—or I don't *want* to stop?" Remind students that rumination makes them angrier but doesn't change the situation. "It is like drinking poison and expecting the other person to die. It hurts only you."

J. **Summary and Homework**

1. Review the definition of mindfulness and how mindfulness can increase focus and enhance our ability to be aware of and control our emotions. Describe the pitfalls of rumination behavior, and review how becoming more mindful can help control this behavior.

2. Assign Hassle Logs for homework. In addition, ask students to practice mindfulness at home:

Tell the students to pick an activity they do every day without noticing. Instead of completing this task on autopilot, ask them to do it one time while being fully aware of their body and their surroundings. For example, while brushing their teeth mindfully, they may notice all the different sensations (e.g., the feel of the brush against their teeth and gums, the smell and taste of the toothpaste, the sounds as they brush).

Session 5: Assertiveness Techniques

A. Collect and Review Hassle Logs and Homework Assignments

Ask if the group noticed anything differently or more intensely when they observed situations with purposeful mindfulness. Discuss with them: "Where is your mind *usually* while you engage in this activity?" Ask about how they felt after doing the mindfulness activity at home.

B. Recap Previous Session

C. Practice Brief Mindfulness Activity to Orient the Group's Attention and Focus

D. Introduce Objectives Effectiveness

(Adapted from *Skills Training Manual for Treating Borderline Personality Disorder* by Marsha M. Linehan [1993a].)

Explain that being effective in a relationship means getting what you want or need from another person (i.e., achieving a goal or objective in the course of an interaction with someone else). This includes making sure your own rights are respected, asking someone to do something in a way that increases the chance that they will do it, and resolving conflicts so that they don't worsen or continue.

E. Introduce Skills to Enhance Objectives Effectiveness

Start with the DEAR MAN objectives effectiveness skills used in dialectical behavior therapy (Linehan, 1993a). Explain that DEAR MAN stands for the following:

1. **Describe**: State the facts about a situation without being judgmental. For example, one can be objective by saying, "This is the third time this week you have borrowed my phone for music!" rather than "You are such a leech! You need to get your *own* music account!"

2. **Express**: Communicate your feelings, thoughts, and opinions about the situation. Don't assume that someone else knows what you believe or how you feel. Expressing yourself clearly can prevent others from misunderstanding you. For example, you might say, "I would love to share my candy with you, but I have only a few left and promised them to Anna, so I can't give you one." This prevents someone from assuming you aren't sharing because you don't like her or because you are selfish.

3. **Assert**: Clearly say what you're asking for or what you are saying no to. Again, don't assume people will know what you mean without clearly

stating it. Remember to say what *you* want or need but not what *others* should do. Saying, "Hey, can I borrow your cell phone?" is much more effective than saying, "Are you using your cell phone?" and hearing no, then follow-up responding with, "Oh, I just wanted to know" and getting angry because the other person did not offer to let you borrow it.

4. **Reinforce**: When someone *does* give you what you have asked for or has responded to you in a positive way, it's important to reward them. "Rewarding" usually means saying positive things back to the person or describing the positive effect their actions have had on you. You can even sometimes reinforce others before they respond to you and include it in your request (e.g., "I will be able to get my work done faster if you let me listen to music on your phone, and then I will be able to help you study for the test sooner!" or "I would really appreciate it if you would help me put this stuff away!").

5. Stay **Mindful**: This is about keeping your attention on your goals for the interaction and not allowing yourself to get sidetracked or distracted onto something else. Techniques for staying focused on your goal will be presented and include the Broken Record, Ignoring, and Escalating Assertion methods.

6. **Appear** confident: Present yourself in such a way that communicates that you are effective and assertive and that your requests deserve respect. Think about posture, eye contact, and how you might use your voice. How would these aspects be different from someone who appears arrogant? How effective is someone who always appears shy?

7. **Negotiate**: This is about adjusting your request or offering to do something in exchange in order to solve the problem or resolve the conflict. You can also turn it around and include the other person, asking them to generate a solution, by asking, "How should we solve this problem?"

Other techniques for achieving objectives:

> *Broken Record*: This response involves calmly expressing oneself over and over. This technique is effective when students can prevent the conversation from becoming loud or aggressive and instead focus on the repetition and persistence.

> *Ignoring*: This technique is useful for keeping focus on the objective and not letting the other person determine the direction of the interaction. When the other person is attacking or making threats, ignoring it will keep the student on track, whereas responding to it will give the other

person control of the conversation. Using Broken Record and Ignoring together can be very effective for not allowing oneself to be diverted from one's goal.

> *Empathic Assertion*: This is a form of assertion that involves sensitive listening on the student's part to the other person's feeling state. This method is particularly useful when dealing with authority figures who are angry. For example, if a staff member complains, "This room is a mess. I can't believe you guys are such slobs! Start cleaning immediately!" the student who learns how to use Empathic Assertion might answer, "I know you're upset with the mess, but we just got back from the rec room and haven't had time to clean up yet." Discuss how the staff member in this situation would have felt better because their feelings were heard.

> *Escalating Assertion*: This is a sequence of responses that increases in assertiveness in order to obtain a desired outcome. Begin with a minimal assertive response, and escalate to a final contract option in which a threat to the other person for noncompliance to original demand is presented. For example: (1) "Please return my cell phone," (2) "I asked you to return my cell phone," (3) "I want my cell phone *now*," and (4) "If you don't give me my cell phone, I will go tell the staff, and they will come and get my cell phone *for* me."

> *Fogging*: This is a technique used to short-circuit an aggressive verbal conflict by confusing the provoker. The individual being provoked should appear to agree with the provoker but not actually agree. For example, the provoker might say, "You are stupid," and the target student might reply, "I *know* you think I'm stupid." Explain to group members that such an agreement does not indicate truth but is rather a way to turn things into a joke. Students can also use their description skills to state plainly (and nonjudgmentally) what is happening instead of responding to the aggression; for example, a student might respond to repeated verbal attacks by saying, "You keep telling me insults, and I keep ignoring them."

F. **Exercise**

Ask for volunteers to role-play the following situations using the listed techniques:

> Please describe to a staff member how you deserve to get the bathroom pass first because you have been waiting the longest and have not been able to use the bathroom all day.

> A person wants to close the window in the room because it is cold, but you are hot; by expressing your feelings or opinions clearly, ask the person to leave the window open.

> Directly assert your wish to eat an apple that your friend does not seem to be eating.

> Reinforce someone for letting you use their cell phone.

> Stay mindful when asking someone to stop talking about your friend by using the Broken Record method when they keep saying different bad things about her.

> Appear confident when telling someone you are not going to let them cheat off your paper during the test next period.

> Negotiate with someone in order to get them to help you study for an exam.

G. Summary and Homework

1. Discuss with students when to use assertive responses rather than withdrawal or aggressive responses. Assertion is optimal when the adolescent is certain of their rights in a situation and when there is a high probability of a nonaggressive, successful outcome to the problematic situation.

   • It is not a good idea to use an assertive response when the individual is not clear about their rights (e.g., the student is asking to go first but isn't sure the other person wasn't there first). An assertion technique also should not be used if there is a good chance that it will lead to further aggression or harm.

2. Assign more Hassle Logs for homework. In addition, ask the students to write down at least two incidents in which they practiced assertiveness.

Session 6: Relationship-Building Techniques

A. Collect and Review Hassle Logs and Homework Assignments

Ask for volunteers to describe examples of practicing assertiveness in their own lives.

B. Recap Previous Session

C. Practice Brief Mindfulness Activity to Orient the Group's Attention and Focus

D. Introduce Relationship Effectiveness

Part of being effective means maintaining or improving a relationship while trying to get what one wants or needs. *Relationship effectiveness* also requires students to contrast and balance immediate goals with long-term relationship objectives. Students can be asked "Is it possible to both get what you need from someone and have that person feel good about giving it to you?"

E. Relationship Effectiveness Skills: GIVE

Introduce the relationship effectiveness skills used in dialectical behavior therapy represented by the acronym "GIVE" (Linehan, 1993a). Explain that GIVE stands for

> Be **Gentle**: Pose the question "Do you respond to others better when they attack, threaten, and judge you or when they approach you in a polite and considerate manner?" This skill is not only about avoiding overly harsh tactics but also about refraining from implicit judgment about what others "should" do.

> Act **Interested**: People will respond more positively to you if they believe that you are interested in where they are coming from. Give the other person the chance to speak about their opinion, and listen to what they have to say.

> **Validate**: Communicate that you recognize the other person's position, difference of opinion, or feelings about the situation. This can be as simple as saying, "I know you have to study for a test tomorrow, so I will make this brief."

> Use an **Easy** manner: This skill is about trying to be upbeat or lighthearted to get someone to work with you on your request. Using an easy manner can be contrasted with putting someone in a hard place, pushing them around, or using guilt trips.

F. Exercise

Ask for group volunteers to practice role plays using GIVE techniques:

1. A friend is telling you about a concert that they went to over the weekend; you two do not share interests in music, so you are unfamiliar with the concert.

2. Have group members come up with a typical parent–child discussion that they can role-play in which GIVE skills are used.

G. Summary and Homework

1. Discuss the importance of using relationships skills to maintain and enhance connections with others.

2. Assign more Hassle Logs for homework. In addition, ask the students to practice GIVE skills in a conversation with a friend or family member this week.

Session 7: Self-Instruction Training

A. Collect and Review Hassle Logs and Homework Assignments

B. Recap Previous Session

C. Practice Brief Mindfulness Activity

D. Introduce Self-Instruction Training

1. Define *reminders* as things we say to ourselves to guide our behavior or to get us to remember certain things. Ask group members to think of specific things they say, for example, to remind themselves to bring certain items to class or to remind themselves of things they need to do when they get home.

2. Give examples of instances where reminders can be used in pressure situations (such as at the foul line during a very close basketball game).

3. Describe how students can implement reminders by recognizing that they are getting angry and then stopping themselves by pausing, kicking back, looking away for a moment, and saying to themselves, "Stay calm." The key components to this sequence are (a) Stop, (b) Press the Pause Button, (c) Kick Back, and (d) Remind.

4. Describe how reminders can also be helpful in situations in which the student has to try to stay calm. Reminders, or internal self-control statements, are key ingredients of increased personal power. Thinking before acting gives students control over their anger arousal and helps them determine their choice in response to provocation.

E. Application of Reminders Procedure: Transitioning From Overt (Outside) to Covert (Inside) Reminders

1. Model the use of overt reminders by role-playing a situation in which one student is cursing out another who is emitting audible reminders in order to ignore these behaviors. Suggest the use of reminders instead of reacting to the direct provocation.

2. Fully describe the substitution procedure, whereby a youth has a choice after recognizing the activating anger trigger. They can either react in an angry or aggressive way—which may lead to receipt of negative consequences—or they can emit covert reminders to remain calm and uninvolved in the conflict situation. Emphasize the personal power inherent in not responding to anger provocation.

   - Demonstrate use of covert reminders, and review rationale for maintaining this level of self-control.

- Emphasize the idea that the timing of reminders is critical. Provide examples of someone who uses reminders before any actual provocation (too soon) and after they have received a punishment for explosive behaviors (too late).

- Discuss candidly, with the students, situations in which they would be unwilling or unlikely to ignore a direct provocation.

F. Exercises

1. Have the group members generate a list of reminders that they can use in those highly charged situations, and write those reminders on the blackboard. Examples include "Slow down," "Take it easy," "Take a deep breath," "Let it go," "Chill out," and "Ignore this."

2. It's Hot in the Middle: Have students choose the best reminders and write them on index cards. Shuffle the cards, and have the students sit in a circle with one student in the middle. Have other students provoke that student, and have the student being provoked practice aloud using the reminder (and any others that student might generate) on the index card. Provocative situations should be generated from Hassle Logs.

G. Summary and Homework

1. Review the concept of reminders and the effective use of reminders.

2. Provide more Hassle Logs. Ask students to write down two instances in which they can practice using reminders.

Session 8: Thinking Ahead

A. Collect and Review Hassle Logs and Homework Assignments

Have the students give one another feedback on how hassles were managed. This will model the use of direct peer social reinforcement for improved anger control outside the therapy room.

B. Recap Previous Session

C. Practice Mindfulness Activity to Orient the Group's Attention and Focus

D. Introduce Thinking Ahead Procedure as Another Self-Control Technique to Use in Conflict or Anger-Provoking Situations

1. Define *Thinking Ahead procedure* as using problem solving and self-instructions to estimate future negative consequences for possible current aggressive response to a conflict situation (e.g., "If I slap her in the face, I will get restriction and not be able to go out this weekend," "If I slap her in the face, I'll get suspended from school and have to go to summer school," "If I start a rumor about her, she might start one about me that will embarrass me," or "If I post this comment on her Instagram, she may retaliate and post something that embarrasses me").

2. Explain Thinking Ahead procedure by stressing the importance of using future negative consequences as a reminder to not get involved in acting-out behaviors, and discuss the relevance of appropriate timing when using the Thinking Ahead procedure.

3. Define *covert* and *overt* consequences of aggressive behavior.

   - Covert examples: people not liking you, people not trusting you, losing your friends, or being burdened by the reputation of acting out so everyone assumes you to be involved in any given conflict.

   - Overt examples: having your privileges withdrawn or being placed in a more restrictive environment.

4. Explain to students that they should remind themselves of negative consequences; stop the possible misbehavior; and substitute an alternative behavior such as deep breaths, assertion techniques, or reminders. This process underscores the principle of *thinking before acting*.

E. Exercises

1. Have the students break into teams and develop a list of covert and overt, short-term and long-term, internal and external punishing consequences for aggressive behavior (e.g., hitting another student, talking back to a

teacher). Have them order the list hierarchically from the least punishing consequence to the most punishing consequence.

2. Have the group sit in a circle, and have them provoke each other. During the provocation, have them use the Thinking Ahead procedure by saying aloud the statement "If I [misbehave] now, then I will [future consequences]."

3. Have two students role-play a provoking event from one of their Hassle Logs. During the role play, have them identify, for the other group members, the course of action they would normally have taken; then have them remind themselves aloud what the negative consequences would be for such a course of action. Have them substitute an alternative behavior (e.g., assertion, reminders), and have them identify which alternative behavior they are using. Have the actors and group discuss the positive consequences of the alternative behavior.

4. Discuss how acting aggressively on the internet or via text message is sometimes easier to do than saying the same thing in person. Describe how posting aggressive comments or saying things in text messages can have worse consequences (e.g., it can be saved or shared with others). Ask for examples from the group.

F. **Summary and Homework**

1. Review Thinking Ahead procedure: Have students identify negative consequences that might occur in the future that they can use to control their present behavior. Also, discuss the future positive consequences for achieving better anger control (e.g., more privileges, improved reputation).

2. Hand out more Hassle Logs. Also ask the students to implement the Thinking Ahead procedure and write about its effectiveness.

Session 9: Problem Solving Training

A. Collect and Review Hassle Logs and Homework Assignments

B. Recap Previous Session

C. Practice Mindfulness Activity to Orient the Group's Attention and Focus

D. Introduce Problem Solving Training

This is the process used to make a choice between anger control alternatives. Emphasize that the following questions cannot be generated unless the student is able to recognize that they are angry and then stop, pause, and think. Present the following sequences to students on a board, and review each step, giving examples from the Hassle Logs the group presented during the session.

1. Problem definition: *What is the hassle?* Identify the activating stimuli, including the provoking stimulus, situational variables, and internal anger cues. Combine all of these components into a clear definition. For example, if an innocent student is accused of stealing money from another student, the problem definition is that the innocent student is getting angry (and experiencing heart palpitations, burning cheeks, etc.) because they have been accused unfairly of stealing.

2. Generation of alternative solutions: *What are my options?* ("What *can* I do?") This phase requires individuals to brainstorm all of the possible responses to the problem situation. The process of brainstorming precludes the evaluation or critique of any responses generated until a later time.

3. Consequence evaluation: *What is my penalty?* ("What will happen if…?") Using methods similar to those incorporated in the Thinking Ahead procedure, identify positive and negative consequences for each response. These consequences should be overt and covert (again: "outside" and "inside," respectively). Identify long- and short-term consequences.

4. Choosing a solution: *What action will I take?* ("What *will* I do?") This phase involves rank ordering all solutions generated according to the desirability/undesirability or severity of the consequences enumerated above. The solution that optimizes positive consequences, minimizes negative consequences, and solves the presenting problem is the one to implement first.

5. Define *self-evaluation* as a method of providing oneself with feedback on how a conflict situation was handled. Self-evaluation responses are reminders that occur after a conflict situation to provide the individual

with immediate feedback on behavior and feelings during the conflict; thus, they can be thought of as "after-reminders." Discuss how positive and negative after-reminders, in hindsight, might have served to affect the behavior that preceded them. (This is a lesson on the process of self-reinforcement.)

6. Feedback: *How did it work?* The final step in the problem solving procedure involves the evaluation of the solution based on its effectiveness in solving the problem. The use of after-reminders should also be prompted at this stage. If a chosen solution is not effective, then a second-choice solution should be implemented.

E. Exercises

1. Where There's a Will, There's a Way: Have the students attempt to generate solutions to a problem in which there are a few or no solutions. The vignette should not have an interpersonal component. For example: "What should Susan do if she is stranded on a highway alone, 20 miles from civilization, and has no cell phone?" The goal of this exercise is for the students to begin to differentiate between problems that really have few solutions and those in which alternatives exist.

2. Using examples from students' Hassle Logs, have the students

   1. Identify the problem as a group.

   2. Break into teams and generate alternative solutions.

   3. Come back to the group and discuss positive and negative consequences of all the possible solutions generated by both groups.

   4. Choose a problem solution by majority vote.

   5. Determine, with your help, the solution's effectiveness.

F. Summary and Homework

1. Review problem solving sequence.

2. Provide additional Hassle Logs, and also ask the students to write down incidents in which they used this sequence to solve a problem.

Session 10: Bullying Prevention—Specific Problem Solving Techniques

A. Collect and Review Hassle Logs and Homework Assignments

B. Recap Previous Session

C. Practice Mindfulness Activity to Orient the Group's Attention and Focus

D. Introduce Bullying Prevention and Relational Aggression

Explain that many of the problems that will be covered in this session have less to do with the types of aggression talked about in previous sessions. Define *relational aggression* as the kind of aggression that happens in social relationships in the form of betrayal, gossip, exclusion, humiliation, and lies. Ask the students to take a moment and think about the following questions:

> Do students in your school belong to cliques?

> Are there leaders and followers in cliques?

> How does someone become part of a clique or get kicked out?

> Does being popular mean that someone is nice?

Exercise:

- Ask the students to generate a list of the positive aspects of friendships. Next, generate a list of things students have noticed that friends do to one another that are mean or disrespectful.

- Ask the students if they can think of reasons why girls, in particular, can have really strong friendships and still do mean things to people who might be considered their friends. Why are some people unwilling to stand up to such treatment?

E. Distinguish Between Good Teasing and Bad Teasing

1. Good/friendly teasing: Explain that the purpose here is to be playful, to relate, and to join. This is different than an intention to do harm.

2. Bad/unfriendly teasing: Explain that the purpose of this type of teasing is to hurt or exclude someone. Unfriendly teasing is often used to put someone down.

F. Exercise: Rumors (see Appendix A: Worksheet 16)

1. Read aloud the following case example to the group:

   Regina and Graciela are good friends and part of the same group of friends in their seventh-grade class. Everyone agrees that Graciela is one of the prettiest girls in school. Lately, Graciela has been getting a lot of attention from

Richard, a popular eighth grader. Regina likes Richard and begins spreading rumors about Graciela. Regina tells people that Graciela thinks she's better than everyone else and even claims that there is a sexual relationship between Richard and Graciela.

2. Generate a discussion with the students by posing the following questions and writing down their responses on the board:

   - What are the facts?
   - What might Graciela be feeling in this situation?
   - How do you think Regina is feeling?
   - Why is Regina behaving this way?
   - If Regina and Graciela don't resolve this problem, what might Graciela learn from the experience?

G. Talking It Out

Ask students whether they think it is possible for Regina and Graciela to work things out. Explain that oftentimes we choose *not* to try and talk things out because we are afraid of losing the friendship or we fear that the other person will turn more people against us. In addition, these situations often involve feelings like jealousy, hurt, and lack of confidence—which feelings can be very hard to admit to having. However, choosing *not* to work things out prevents us from having an honest relationship. Introduce the steps to talk out a conflict, and use the case example above to illustrate.

1. Step 1: Preparation

   - Ask students to write down the facts of the situation with all of the details (when it happened, who said what, etc.). Then have them write down how they felt during the incident, how they are feeling now, and what they want to happen.

   - Ask students to write down what they want to say to the other person and practice it in front of a mirror. Remind them about objectives effectiveness and relationship effectiveness skills (DEAR MAN and GIVE) when deciding what to say. Also, remind them to pay attention to body posture, voice tone, and eye contact. Students may choose to practice with a trusted adult and ask for feedback.

2. Step 2: Confrontation

   - Explain that students should not approach the other person in front of their friends. Rather, they should choose a place and time in which both parties will feel safe to talk. Asking for a private conversation or inviting an adult to be present for the confrontation may be helpful.

3. Exercise:

- Have students practice by generating ideas about how Graciela might go about the preparation to confront Regina. Write responses on the board.

- Role-play the confrontation. Have student observers offer feedback.

- Ask for examples of celebrity feuds (musicians, athletes, etc. who have publicly bullied each other over social media). Discuss the role that attention may play in why some people frequently find themselves bullying others.

H. Apologizing

1. Explain to the students that apologizing can be a difficult skill to master but is a very important one for maintaining and improving relationships. Apologizing is a mature gesture that requires them to recognize how they have negatively impacted someone else and take responsibility for their actions. How do they make an apology? Describe how an apology is only effective when

- it is genuine—meaning there is a real understanding of the hurt caused, and the person making the apology is sincere (forced apologies are generally not effective)

- the person making the apology speaks only about their actions, without adding any insults or excuses

2. Exercise: Have students role-play Regina's apology to Graciela, and have the observers offer feedback.

I. The Power of Words: Verbal Aggression

1. Ask students why they think certain words have so much power, such as the words "bitch" or "slut." Who gets called these words and why?

2. Ask students whether they monitor or change their behavior in fear of being labeled with a powerful word. Discuss what behaviors would elicit these labels from others.

J. Introduce Self-Respect Effectiveness (Linehan, 1993a)

Explain that this is about keeping respect for themselves in their interactions with others. This includes respecting their own beliefs and values. State that skills for self-respect include the following:

➤ *Being fair to yourself and others.* Self-respect is not just about watching out for yourself—it is actually about being and acting like someone worthy of your respect. Not being fair or taking advantage of others makes it hard to respect yourself.

➤ *Remembering your values and acting accordingly.* Don't do something that goes against what you believe just to obtain a short-term goal, such as getting someone to like you. Maintain your integrity by sticking to your own moral code.

➤ *Being truthful with others.* This means avoiding lying and exaggerations. It may seem like occasional lying is not a big deal; however, over time you will come to see yourself as dishonest, and your goal is to be the person you want to respect. These skills foster self-respect, but it's good to remember that respect from others comes naturally when you have respect in *yourself.*

K. Summary and Homework

1. Review bullying prevention skills.

2. Homework: Remind students to complete Hassle Logs after conflicts. Also, ask them to complete Worksheet 18 (Friendship Inventory) to reflect on their own values regarding friendships.

Session 11: Program Review

A. Collect and Review Hassle Logs and Homework Assignments

B. Practice Mindfulness Activity to Orient the Group's Attention and Focus

C. Program Review

Before the session, write the name of each skill taught in the program on a separate index card. When the session begins, ask each student to select one index card at random. Give the students a few minutes to think about how to describe/define the strategy for using the skill card, how to demonstrate the strategy, and when the best time/situation to implement the strategy is. The students, using the outline above, will discuss the skill they chose with the group. Cards should include at least 10 skills (Take Three, Kick Back, Mindfulness, DEAR MAN, GIVE, Broken Record, Fogging, Reminders, Thinking Ahead, Problem Solving, ABCs, Empathic Assertion, Escalating Assertion, Refuting Aggressive Beliefs). Review of each skill should include the following:

> ➤ Deep breaths: Remind students about their physiological cues and how the Deep Breathing technique can be used to reduce tension and stress, redirect their attention away from external provoking stimuli to internal control, and provide a time delay before making a choice regarding how to respond.

> ➤ Concept of ABCs:

> • *Antecedents* or *activating events* are provoking stimuli. Overt (outside) activating events are situational variables in one's environment that provoke anger. Covert (inside) activating events are physiological states, such as fatigue.

>> » *Triggers* are provoking stimuli. *Direct triggers* are direct aversive provocations by another person. These may occur in verbal or nonverbal form. *Indirect triggers* are the adolescent's misinterpretation or misattribution of events—the result of a faulty appraisal system. Indirect triggers may also include observed injustice or unfairness.

>> » *Faulty reminders* or *faulty beliefs* need to be replaced with statements directing the student to let go of personalized anger and look at other ways to view the situation less aggressively.

> • *Behavior* is the individual's actual reaction to the provoking stimuli, which can involve a variety of cognitive, physiological, covert, and overt responses.

- *Consequences* are events that happen as a result of controlling or not controlling anger. Consequences can be either rewarding or punishing.

➤ *Mindfulness*, or remaining aware and present in the moment, can help control anger reactions and help reduce rumination behaviors.

➤ *Assertion techniques* include objectives effectiveness and relationship effectiveness skills (DEAR MAN, GIVE, Broken Record, Ignoring, Fogging).

➤ *Reminders* are things we say to ourselves (overtly and covertly) to guide our behavior or to help us remember certain things.

➤ The *Thinking Ahead procedure* is another type of reminder that utilizes problem solving and self-instruction to estimate future negative consequences for current misbehavior to a conflict situation.

➤ In *Problem Solving*, the student should think through (a) *What is the hassle?* ("What is the problem?"), (b) *What are my options?* ("What *can* I do?"), (c) *What are the penalties?* ("What will happen if…?"), (d) *What action will I take?* ("What *will* I do?"), and (e) *What is my feedback?* ("How did it work?").

D. Discuss Situational and Personal Elements That Would Help the Student Determine Which Strategy to Use

1. Introduce barbs: A *barb* is a provocation statement made directly to the target adolescent, preceded by warnings in warm-up situations until the actual training one. The adolescent is issued a warning first ("I'm going to barb you"), then the barb is delivered (e.g., "Why were you watching TV when your privileges have been revoked?"). The person giving the barb notes the adolescent's response and gives both positive and constructive feedback. Gradually, the barbs should more closely come to approximate realistic inquires made by staff members, parents, or others in the adolescent's environment. If possible, these barbs should also be delivered by carefully selected others in more natural environments. These challenges should occur spontaneously with graduating intensity.

   Initially, the group leader should barb the students so that they get used to the procedure. Because this is Phase 1, all of the barbs should start with a warning. Role plays can also be done in which group members barb one another. Those members watching can identify which anger management skills were exhibited.

2. Ask students to describe in detail several conflict situations that have occurred. Ask them to describe the various anger management techniques

they used during the provocations. Another option is to have the students role-play several scenes using the anger management skills they have learned: Pass a hat filled with index cards that identify the various anger management techniques. Whichever technique is selected, the student has to try to use that skill in their role play. Other students observing have to guess which technique is being implemented.

E. Closing Remarks

1. Provide each student with feedback on

   - their cooperation during the program

   - their performance during the exercises and role plays

   - their enthusiasm and/or interest in various components of the program

   - their motivation for change (being on time, completing homework assignments and Hassle Logs, etc.)

   - their observable changes in behavior, including any anecdotal observations from another person involved with student

2. Let the student know what you have learned by participating in the group, and tell the student that you enjoyed working with them.

3. Ask each group member to review their participation. Have each of them give self-evaluative praise statements regarding their participation and improvement in anger management. Prompt students to reinforce observed changes in each other.

4. Prepare students for situations in which their newly acquired anger management skills may not work out as they hope or expect. Leaders can role-play "failed" scenarios in order to prepare group members for future frustrations.

5. Plan for a follow-up or booster session.

F. Administer Posttest Questionnaires/Assessments (If Applicable)

Session 12: Follow-Up/Booster Session

A. Collect and Review Any Additional Hassle Logs and Assignments Completed Since the End of the Formal Program

B. Practice Mindfulness Activities to Orient the Group's Attention and Focus

C. Program Review

Before the session, write the name of each skill taught in the program on a blackboard. When the session begins, ask each student to pick a skill and (a) describe/define the strategy, (b) demonstrate the strategy, and (c) discuss when the best time/situation to implement the strategy is.

The skills taught include

- Deep Breathing
- Concept of ABCs
  - Antecedents
    - » Triggers
    - » Faulty Reminders
  - Behavior
  - Consequences
- Mindfulness and Avoiding Rumination
- Assertiveness Techniques (DEAR MAN, GIVE, etc.)
- Reminders
- Thinking Ahead
- Problem Solving:
  1. What is the problem?
  2. What *can* I do?
  3. What will happen if…?
  4. What *will* I do?
  5. How did it work?

Ask students to describe in detail several conflict situations that have occurred. Ask them to describe the various anger control techniques they used during the provocations.

D. Closing Remarks

1. Provide each student with feedback on

   - their cooperation during the program

   - their performance during exercises and roles

   - their enthusiasm and/or interest in various components of the program

   - their motivation for change (being on time, completing homework assignments and Hassle Logs, etc.)

   - their observable changes in behavior, including any anecdotal observations from other persons involved with the student

2. Ask students to give one another feedback in terms of positive change.

3. Let each student know what the group leaders have learned by participating in the group and that you have enjoyed working with each student.

4. Ask each group member to review their participation and any change since the program ended. Have each give self-evaluative praise statements regarding their participation and improvement in anger control. Prompt students to reinforce observed changes in each other.

5. Ask how mindfulness activities may have helped change awareness of experiences. Encourage group members to continue practicing mindfulness in their daily lives.

6. Generalization and maintenance: Through group discussion, review situations/events in which anger management led to a positive outcome. Also review situations in which their newly learned skills did not lead to a positive outcome. Brainstorm alternative responses.

7. Wrap-up: Thank students for coming, and ask them each to be a mentor to a friend who might benefit from learning anger management skills.

E. Administer Posttest Questionnaires/Assessments (If Applicable)

Chapter 5

Implementation Issues and Recommendations

School and Community Support

Mihalic and Irwin (2003) reported that amid intense efforts to find empirically validated treatment programs for violent youth, little was known about how to effectively implement these programs in real-world settings. Their analysis of the published literature in this area revealed that research on youth-violence programs focused on outcomes over process and failed to detail factors such as the impact of treatment fidelity on outcomes and implementation factors that contributed to program effectiveness.

Some administrative aspects within schools or agencies were identified as important factors in successful implementation of violence-prevention programs (Mihalic & Irwin, 2003). Specifically, sites with "administrative support, clear lines of authority, structural stability and financial support" were able to ensure core components of the programs were properly implemented (Mihalic & Irwin, 2003, p. 324). This suggests that proper implementation of treatment programs requires more than just administrative approval—it necessitates administrative support throughout the process. According to Langley et al. (2010), who discussed barriers to effective implementation of evidence-based mental health practices in schools, a lack of support by school administrators and teachers was one of the major barriers identified by successful *and* unsuccessful implementers. Before beginning a plan to run a TAME group in your setting, you might want to assess your organization's "readiness for change." Glisson et al. (2008) identified several readiness factors in a Readiness to Change scale. The first factor was the "fit" with the services already offered in the agency, and the second was the dimension of infrastructure support that included the commitment of resources to make certain that the TAME program would be successful. These are just a few of the barriers that should be addressed far before the mental health clinician begins to consider which students might make good candidates for the TAME intervention.

TAME groups conducted in school or residential settings may benefit from educating program officials and staff prior to starting the group. This may help group participants generalize the skills learned in the TAME group into the school or residential setting. Program staff can be asked to support TAME by encouraging participants to complete homework assignments and Hassle Logs. Attendance to TAME groups is likely to be highest when the treatment receives support from school administrators and/or residential staff. Results from Mihalic and Irwin (2003) were consistent with previous research by Fullan (1992), which suggests that school staff and administrations that recognize the larger purpose of implementing new treatment programs in the school are better able to adhere to the program's procedures and express greater commitment to the program.

Among anger management programs conducted in school settings, one of the common anger triggers expressed by group participants is insensitive or provoking teacher/counselor behavior. This is consistent with findings by Sportsman et al. (2010) in a study of anger management program implementation in an elementary school discussed previously in the literature review. Sportsman et al. also found that students experienced strong anger reactions regarding interactions with their teachers. TAME programs implemented in school settings should have parallel professional development seminars for teachers or other professionals regarding the development of healthy relationships with their students to address this common concern.

Fullan (1992) reported that effective treatment implementation in school settings cannot be obtained without community support. A treatment program cannot be effective if it differs from or contradicts the school culture in which it is implemented. Therefore, Fullan suggested that the larger community must be informed of the nature of the problem and the need for such a program in the school. Implementation of the TAME program in school settings should be preceded by community education about increasing youth violence and the need for anger management programs for at-risk adolescents. The lack of community support, involvement, and education about the use of TAME may be especially relevant when racial and socioeconomic differences exist between group leaders and the community from which the participants are recruited. Group leaders should be aware that changing attitudes and/or behaviors in the direction taught by TAME may be inconsistent with the local culture in a way that could result in the participant becoming less socially acceptable in their peer group and even reduce their safety in some situations. Cultural sensitivity and awareness are important factors for any treatment program.

How to Implement TAME in Your School or Agency

Accommodations for Group Sessions

TAME groups should be conducted in physical spaces that are quiet and with limited distractions. The tendency toward impulsivity and attention problems is high among angry and aggressive youth; therefore, environments with multiple distractions (e.g., Case Example #1) make it difficult for TAME participants to remain focused on the group discussion and may make mindfulness activities especially difficult. The physical space in which groups are conducted should be large enough for all group participants to move around during role plays and other activities. Several TAME group activities require participants to break up into smaller groups for discussion or to plan for role plays and games. In order to maximize group participation, adequate space to divide into groups and act out role plays should be considered.

Reinforcers and Motivators Appropriate to the Group

Adolescents with anger management issues are likely to have a history of non-compliance and/or inattentive behavior. Many adolescents with anger-related issues have a history of more easily gaining access to attention from adults and peers for negative behaviors than positive ones. This long history of being reinforced for negative behaviors may not require more than just positive attention and praise from group leaders to be overcome. In many cases, an additional reinforcement system is necessary to increase the adolescent's motivation to attend sessions, actively participate in the group discussions and role plays, and complete homework assignments. During the assessment phase, group leaders should include questions about possible motivators in the interview of the caregiver and the adolescent. It is important that possible rewards for compliance and participation are acceptable and appropriate for the cognitive level of the group. Reinforcement systems, such as a token economy, can be established at the individual or group level and may include a combination of both. For example, group participants may earn individual tokens for their behavior and be working toward a personalized reinforcer, while a simultaneous group-level contingency is in place in which the entire group's performance in session determines whether or not they will earn a prespecified reinforcer at the end of the therapy. Individual contingencies have the benefit of being personalized for the individual but increase the level of resources needed to be effectively implemented in most settings. Reinforcement systems based on the individual may be best applied in structured, residential settings in which token systems already exist to promote behavior change. When TAME groups are run in these settings, participation in group sessions and completion of homework assignments can be added to the existing reinforcement plan.

Group contingencies may be more easily implemented in smaller settings. These kinds of interventions have the benefit of being able to address behavioral and motivational issues with multiple individuals at the same time while promoting group cooperation toward a mutual goal. Group contingencies acknowledge individuals who display prosocial behaviors, but selection of the appropriate type of group contingency is necessary to avoid negative outcomes. Among the three types of group contingencies (independent, interdependent, and codependent), independent group contingencies may be preferable at the onset of treatment because the likelihood of negative peer pressure or scapegoating is low. However, interdependent group contingencies promote positive peer pressure and cooperation at the highest level and may be more appropriate once the group has developed a level of cohesion. Group leaders would ideally fade from one form of group contingency to the interdependent group contingency over the course of the TAME treatment in order to gain the maximal benefits of using this form of reinforcement. For example, a group leader may initially present an independent group contingency system in which all members of the group are working toward a common goal (e.g., a pizza party at the end of Session 3) and each individual may earn access to the reinforcer based on their own behavior in the group. The second reinforcer (e.g., an ice cream party at the end of Session 7) may use an interdependent group contingency in which access to the reinforcer is determined by the performance of the group as a whole. There exists the risk that one individual might sabotage the reward for everyone, but the potential for prosocial peer pressure and a motivation toward cooperation may outweigh the potential pitfalls of this approach.

Using Worksheets, Homework, and Hassle Logs

TAME groups incorporate verbal discussions, physical role plays and games, and written content. TAME worksheets and Hassle Logs are designed to require simple reading skills and minimal effort. The use of worksheets in groups allows participants a form of visual guide with which to supplement verbal discussions of key points. Group participants should be encouraged to take notes on their worksheets during the group sessions in order to customize the content to their respective experiences.

Hassle Logs (described in detail in Chapter 3) provide an opportunity for adolescent group participants to self-monitor their reactions to provocation between sessions. These simple and quick records of the daily "hassles" that contribute to anger-related difficulties can be used in discussions and role plays. In this way, Hassle Logs allow each TAME group to be customized to the experiences of its participants; examples directly generated from the current, real-life hassles of the adolescents in the group may likely be more interesting and meaningful learning experiences. The act of filling out Hassle Logs between sessions has the additional benefit of reminding adolescents of the material covered in TAME groups and prompting them to stop and reflect on provoking situations to assess their responses' effectiveness. This moment of self-assessment promotes increased mindfulness and may help the adolescent address similar hassles more effectively.

Worksheets and Hassle Logs can be collected over the course of the TAME program to provide a physical reference to the compilation of skills developed over the course of treatment. Worksheets and Hassle Logs may also be used for reference in booster sessions or concurrent individual therapy sessions.

Homework assignments are commonly used in cognitive behavioral treatments to provide skill generalization into the natural environment. TAME homework assignments encourage participants to implement the content and skills used in the group sessions. The adolescent's discussions, in subsequent sessions, of their experiences with homework assignments allow the group participant to share their successes (or failures) with implementing the strategies described. Group leaders and other group participants then have an opportunity to provide positive praise and feedback.

Recommended Group Size and Group Readiness

TAME groups are recommended to consist of approximately eight participants. This number is considered ideal because it will allow the group members time to actively participate in the group discussions. Groups that are too large may be distracting and will not allow for the level of intimacy desired to facilitate active participation and in vivo problem solving. Groups that are too small may create difficulties when implementing in-session activities. Some in-session activities require the group to be divided into two teams; thus, a minimum of six participants overall is required.

Prior to starting TAME groups, leaders should assess readiness for group participation and willingness to participate in treatment. Intake assessments should include motivational assessments of potential group participants to determine if students are motivated and oriented to the group approach.

Group Leaders and Session Length

TAME groups should ideally be conducted, at a minimum, in 45- to 50-minute sessions. Due to the impulsivity and attentional difficulties common among adolescents with anger control problems, group sessions that are too long may contribute to additional behavior problems. Extended group sessions can be helpful in the development of group cohesion with older, more mature group participants. Younger, less mature youth should be limited to groups fewer than 60 minutes in order to maximize the amount of material that is digested in one session.

It is recommended that there is no longer than one week between TAME sessions. This will allow participants to process the information learned in group and practice new skills in real-life settings. However, more frequent group sessions may be preferred with younger, less mature group members. Biweekly groups may be more easily facilitated in schools and residential programs.

Having two therapists/group leaders is also recommended. Coleaders allow for in vivo role plays of situations. The use of two therapists also provides increased opportunities for feedback and commenting throughout the group. Specifically, with impulsive adolescents, it may be helpful to have group leaders alternate between presenting the content and monitoring the behavior of the group members. When possible, group leaders of opposite sexes may be preferable because it will allow group members to observe adults of both sexes acting in a controlled manner and modeling anger control techniques. Opposite-sex group leaders may allow for enhanced discussions about gender differences in anger expression and management. Group leaders can consider older adolescents who have successfully completed the TAME curriculum as coleaders, thus providing a more proximal role model.

Addressing Lateness, Absences, and Missing Homework

Group members should be advised of the importance of attending each session on time and completing homework assignments. Lateness, absences, and missing homework should all be viewed as impeding the therapeutic process for the participant and possibly other group members. When these issues occur, group leaders should start by exploring and evaluating reasons for noncompliance. Identifying and addressing these issues as early as possible is advisable. At times, group participants may need to be advised of the rationale for attending sessions on time and completing assignments. Possible misunderstandings regarding requirements should be addressed, and participants should be reminded that failure to complete assignments might lead to restricted ability to participate in role plays. Token programs or group reinforcers may be helpful in preventing or reducing noncompliance behaviors. Continued lateness, noncompliance with requirements, or oppositional behavior in groups may require group leaders to dismiss some participants from the group in order to maintain optimal learning environments for the remaining group participants.

Staff Training and Treatment Fidelity

There are a number of key considerations when planning for TAME implementation, which are more specific to the practitioner factors and training methods identified by Ruzek and Rosen (2009) as crucial in ensuring effective implementation of CBT interventions for youth. Although the TAME manual is written in a manner that makes it easy to follow and includes all necessary worksheets, the level of training of the group leader(s) should be considered. In general, those who will be responsible for the TAME program should be well versed in the CBT model of behavior change and have a basic understanding of psychoeducational approaches to skill development and affect regulation strategies. Attending preliminary training in these areas and/or seeking out clinical supervision of these areas is a start, but receiving supervision or consultation with a senior practitioner or expert is advised. Starting a new group intervention can be challenging, and peer support and/or working with perhaps another mental health professional as a coleader the first time can be helpful.

Fidelity has to do with the degree to which the treatment as written (described and prescribed in the TAME treatment manual) was indeed the program that was actually provided to the youth selected to receive services. Although many mental health providers read treatment manuals, they are not often fully trained or supervised (or certified) in providing evidence-based treatments. It is likely that competent and reasonable practicing professionals pick and choose features of the TAME program that they see as holding promise for particular settings or particular youth. Implementation of selected parts of TAME would likely not meet the rigorous research or clinical standards needed to evaluate treatment fidelity; however, any implementation should consider this challenge: *Was the TAME program implemented the way it was written?* Fidelity is typically determined by someone observing or checking tapes of actual treatment sessions for adherence to the written treatment manual. For TAME, we have provided a session checklist for an estimate of fidelity for each session administered (see Appendix D for fidelity checklists).

Treatment fidelity is not the same as treatment quality: Treatment quality refers to an expert judgment. When one is concerned with quality assurance, it takes an expert to review audio and video recordings of sessions to make quality judgments. It may be that implementation in a particular setting requires a look at treatment quality, which certainly is enhanced if any pre-to-post data has been collected to examine outcomes.

When implemented, a living treatment manual permits therapist creativity and is not rule bound—there is room for flexibility and individualization. However, the treatment is nevertheless provided within the prescribed strategic approach. The manual permits and suggests how the intervention strategies can be tailored to the varied presenting problems within the target goal of managing anger while also endorsing sensitivity to individual youth and context factors. Ideally, manuals are capable of being evaluated for treatment outcomes and are implemented with fidelity, even though clinical needs result in a certain flexibility.

Staff Issues When Working With Angry and Aggressive Youth: Risk and Therapeutic Alliance Issues

Part of the presentation of anger management difficulties is often an angry attitude and disinterest in participation. Actually, one of the typical characteristics of those with anger and aggression problems is the tendency to externalize blame and resist typical intervention efforts. In fact, aggressive youth are the least likely to request mental health assistance as they believe that nothing is attributable to them and that therapy is not helpful. (In the assessment section, we report on an inventory [ATAMS] that assesses attitudes toward anger management.) Establishing an agreement to participate, fully engaging angry participants, and managing heightened emotions during role play practice are all challenges to a successful implementation of a TAME program.

Co-Occurring Parenting Groups

Parental education about the TAME program and co-occurring parent training may also contribute to better treatment outcomes. Informing parents about the skills discussed in TAME may contribute to reinforcement of these concepts in the home and greater awareness, by the parents, of changes in adolescent behavior. Given the literature on parental interactions and the intergenerational transmission of emotion regulation dysfunction, parents of the adolescent TAME participants may benefit from parent training by learning new ways of managing their own anger, disciplining their adolescent, and avoiding the coercive parenting techniques that contribute to antisocial behavior. Parental involvement in treatment programs should not be limited to discussing factors within the family that are thought to be pathogenic. Instead, focusing on other parental concerns like caregiver strain (e.g., difficulties associated with caring for a child with behavioral problems) is also an important factor when considering transporting research-based programs to real-world settings.

Facilitation Strategies and Troubleshooting Group Behavior Problems

In nonclinical groups of children with behavioral disorders like ODD/CD, comorbidity with ADHD is high. Bögels et al. (2008) reported that among clinical populations, "ODD/CD without ADHD is rare" (p. 194). Information processing problems may be the underlying factor that contributes to inattention and impulsivity. Given these factors, clinicians implementing anger management groups should expect and prepare for attentional difficulties and impulsive responding in group sessions. In order to address these common concerns, the TAME program includes worksheets designed to help group participants focus on the material being discussed. The worksheets provide inattentive youth with a visual reference of the content of each session, increasing the youth's ability to rejoin the group discussion if they "zoned out" for any period of time. The worksheets prompt note-taking to further engage the group participant in the core content of the session. Each worksheet can be used for review in future sessions, as part of the recap, or during booster sessions. The completion of all worksheets thus creates an "anger management coping strategies" reference book to which group members can refer in the future (e.g., in co-occurring individual sessions). The goal of these worksheets is to provide youth with a visual prompt for staying on task in the group discussion and to develop a reference book of newly acquired skills.

TAME groups conducted in school settings may more easily adapt to the use of the worksheets. Groups in clinical settings may require a greater orientation to the purpose of worksheets during the group sessions. TAME groups with youth that have cognitive limitations (e.g., reduced reading level) may require revision of the group material to include simplified worksheets and more of a focus on hands-on activities and interactive teaching strategies to maintain group attention.

The following are additional facilitation strategies that should be considered with implementing the TAME protocol. Group leaders should provide immediate, frequent, and salient feedback for positive and negative behaviors. Considering the attention difficulties and behavioral history of the participants, feedback that is in the moment and specific to the behaviors displayed is most effective in establishing structure to the group environment. Group leaders should consider adjunctive token programs to increase positive participation during sessions. The token programs can be designed to include individual or group-level incentives based on each group member's participation.

Group leaders should praise those who volunteer and reward even minimal attempts to use anger management strategies. Leaders should focus on creating a culture of active involvement without fear of "looking stupid." Group members should be reminded that anger management skill use requires practice and the expectation is not that they will implement each skill perfectly from the beginning. Hassle Logs may provide group members with opportunities to share successes and review unsuccessful attempts at using the TAME coping strategies. Group leaders may (a) consider providing scripts for role plays to reduce performance anxiety and/or (b) model role plays in order to demonstrate to group members how to make use of the in-session activity. Group leaders should consider using imperfect modeling of new skills in order to generate discussion and make role plays as consistent with "real-life" attempts as possible.

TAME group leaders should avoid unrealistic, positive reframing of problems discussed by group members, which may increase skepticism of the profession and marginalize some group members. For example, a group member who frequently provides examples of ways in which a parent uses hostile language and extreme consequences in response to problematic behavior would be better served by a group leader who acknowledges that perhaps the parent has anger issues of their own (thereby validating the youth's experience) than by reframing the experience as instances of the parent simply "having a bad day."

Group leaders can expect that youth attending TAME groups may reject scenarios provided in the manual. Although the TAME program was updated to include modern examples of common adolescent problems, no program can be expected to resonate with all youth. Hassle Logs provide group leaders with a wealth of behavioral instances that can be used in these situations to revise or expand upon given activities. Youth-generated examples are likely to be more relevant and engaging scenarios for all group members and should be used whenever possible. Additionally, role plays and activities may be modified based on group composition. Groups of all-female participants may benefit from increased discussion and role plays involving relational aggression. Groups composed of older adolescents in serious relationships may focus on anger in dating relationships and domestic violence concerns.

Finally, group leaders should be prepared to respond to common misconceptions about aggression and fighting. Shetgiri et al. (2015) studied the differences between adolescents described as "fighters" and their nonfighting counterparts. The findings suggest that differences in cognitive distortions related to aggression likely determine the differences in behavior. Adolescents who fight view aggression as the only option; are more likely to report that fights establish respect among peer groups; and are exposed to greater violence in their communities, media, and music. These adolescents are also more likely to get conflicting messages from their families about aggressive behavior. When conducting TAME groups, group leaders should be aware of these factors and confront these cognitive distortions when they are discussed or alluded to in group sessions. Additionally, Goldstein et al. (2013) found that girls often endorse the misconception that relational aggression (e.g., exclusion, starting rumors) has fewer negative consequences than physical aggression. In TAME groups with girls, it is recommended that group members explicitly confront this common misconception and remind group participants of the damaging long-term consequences of relational aggression, including loss of friendships and other negative consequences, to important relationships.

Summary

In summary, although there are many issues that require careful consideration prior to the implementation of a TAME program, all of the above suggestions are designed to ensure the success of the intervention for angry and aggressive teens. TAME has not yet received sufficient outcomes data to determine a level of empirical evidence needed to designate the program as evidence based; however, mental health clinicians working in schools and clinical settings with this population are encouraged to gather data and examine both the outcomes and the process of TAME implementation. The following section provides a list of several administrative and clinical issues to think through before including TAME as a psychosocial intervention program in any context.

Administrative and Clinical Issues in Anger Management Training in School Settings

General Program Administration

- Do you have administrative support for structure and implementation of program and allocation of resources?
- Have you considered ethical issues related to screening and identification of group members, consent to treatment, and confidentiality?
- Articulation and championing of goals and objectives of TAME programming.

Structure of TAME Program

- Screening and assessment of youth relative to clinical and risk status and readiness to change.

- What measures will be used for a pre-to-post evaluation?

- Group membership: Decisions need to be made about same-sex groups, level of risk and/or aggressiveness, readiness for group intervention versus individual treatment, and prior relationships with group members.

- Involvement of teachers, staff, and parents: What are their roles and responsibilities?

Qualified Staff

- Select motivated and capable staff as intervention leaders.

- Ensure experience, skills, credentials, and availability.

- Provide ongoing training, supervision, and technical assistance.

Treatment Fidelity

- Protocol adherence: Is TAME really being implemented in the recommended training sequence?

- Dosage flexibility: How long are the sessions, and how often and with what frequency do they occur?

- Quality of program delivery: Who is implementing the program? How have they been trained and supervised?

Clinical Issues

- Will TAME be used as an adjunct to other mental health treatment?

- Overarousal and discharge in role play and group discussion needs management.

- Ethical issues related to confidentiality and group dynamics.

- Transfer and generalization of skills; homework compliance, reinforcement procedures, and booster sessions.

- Should there be an associated parent/family component?

Section Three

Section Three

Chapter 6

Initial Evaluation of TAME in a Middle School Setting

Introduction

Anger-related problems and increasing aggression and violence among American youth necessitate the development of an effective anger management program. Research on anger-related problems suggests that individuals in need of anger management treatment are more likely to have problem solving issues, make hostile attribution biases, make positive evaluations of the outcome of aggression, have poor affective social competence and inhibitory control, and have antagonistic personality profiles. Treatment that targets the skills training, cognitive tendencies, and emotion regulation instruction supported by the literature on anger control is needed.

Adolescence is a particularly important time in the development of skills to manage feelings of anger, given the move toward adult responsibilities and intensifying emotional experiences. Adolescents with anger and aggression problems are at increased risk for physical injuries, psychological disorders (e.g., anxiety, depression, suicidal ideation, homicidal ideation), criminality, poor academic performance, drug and alcohol abuse, health problems (e.g., cardiovascular disease), dysfunctional relationships, and occupational problems. Anger in adolescents is often associated with exposure to strong negative emotions, family members who lack skills regarding emotional arousal, exposure to domestic violence, and caregivers with poor parenting practices (e.g., lack of supervision, aggressive styles of discipline).

The most common treatments for anger problems in adolescents are contingency management, anger replacement training, and anger management training. Contingency management programs involve reinforcement of appropriate behaviors and use of coping skills but are generally only effective in structured settings in which access to reinforcers is well controlled. Anger replacement training is a cognitive behavioral intervention that consists of three components: prosocial skills, anger control, and moral reasoning training. Anger management training includes skills training about the cognitive, physiological, and behavioral components of anger; situational triggers; adaptive and maladaptive functions of anger; and the concept of self-responsibility in response to provocation.

The purpose of this study was to collect preliminary evidence on the effectiveness of the TAME program developed by Feindler and Gerber (2008). This enhanced anger management program includes components that address the cognitive and social skills deficits identified by the research literature as common among individuals with anger problems. TAME also includes DBT concepts that address the emotional dysregulation of adolescents with anger-related difficulties. Hassle Logs are used to actively monitor elements of anger-provoking situations and encourage immediate self-evaluations.

The main hypothesis of this study was that adolescents, caregivers, and teachers would promote improvement in anger control skills from pre- to post-treatment.

Procedure

A sample of 20 middle school students (ages 13 and 14) was recruited from a charter school in New York. Students attending this school resided in an economically disadvantaged neighborhood. The school population consisted of over 700 students, 94% of whom were African American. The remaining students consisted mostly of first-generation Hispanic immigrants. For participation in this study, students were referred for anger management by the social work department at their school. Individuals with current substance abuse, psychosis, or developmental disorders were excluded from participation and subsequently not referred by the social work department, which prescreened study participants for these factors. Parental consent and adolescent assent were received prior to inclusion in the study. The sample of 20 students consisted mostly of females (75%) and was mostly African American or biracial (90%). Each student was randomly assigned to the treatment or wait-list control group, with the exception of three participants who could not be randomly assigned due to scheduling conflicts.

The treatment group proceeded through an eight-session TAME treatment program. This earlier version of the TAME manual was a shorter treatment package that incorporated traditional anger management topics (e.g., recognizing emotions and triggers, problem solving skills) and interpersonal effectiveness skills training typically used in DBT treatments developed by Marsha Linehan

(1993b). In-session role plays, homework assignments, and Hassle Logs were included in the treatment sessions. The program did not include the mindfulness training described in the current TAME manual. The wait-list control group completed the same TAME treatment program after an 8-week delay.

Data were collected from each adolescent group participant, one caregiver, and one teacher. Caregivers completed a demographics questionnaire and the parent form of the Behavior Assessment Scales for Children, Second Edition (BASC-2). Adolescent group participants completed the self-report form of the BASC-2, How I Think Questionnaire (HIT-Q), and Multidimensional School Anger Inventory (MSAI). Teachers completed the teacher-report form of the BASC-2. Data were collected at three time points: Assessment 1 (pre-intervention for both groups), Assessment 2 (pre-intervention control group, post-intervention treatment group), and Assessment 3 (post-intervention control group).

Group leaders were doctoral-level clinical psychology students, one of whom was conducting this research as part of her dissertation research. Treatment fidelity was evaluated by using checklists developed by the research based on the TAME manual session outlines. All group leaders were supervised weekly by a licensed psychologist throughout the treatment implementation.

A mixed model statistical analysis was used to evaluate the significance of pre-to-post changes on each of the outcome measures. While a repeated measures analysis of variance (ANOVA) might typically be used to measure significant differences between the three time points before and after the implementation of the treatment, a mixed model approach is more sophisticated and allows participants with missing data to be included in the analysis.

For the purpose of evaluating the treatment effect in this investigation, a "focused" or "targeted" set of contrasts are estimated and ultimately combined to provide one overall estimate of the effectiveness of TAME for each of the dependent variables studied. A contrast is a linear combination of two or more factor level means (Gravetter & Wallnau, 2007). Contrast A evaluates whether there is any evidence of change, consistent with expectation, in the experimental group from Time 1 to Time 2, during which the group participants were exposed to TAME. The second contrast, Contrast B, evaluates this same question for the wait-list control group from Time 2 to Time 3, during which these participants were exposed to the intervention. A third contrast, Contrast C, tests for change in the wait-list control group from Time 1 to Time 2. No change is expected in this control condition. Finally, the best evaluation of treatment efficacy is measured by Contrast D, in which Contrasts A and B are "averaged" and compared to an estimate of change in the wait-list control group when it was not exposed to the treatment program (Contrast C). This contrast is best represented by the following statement:

$$\text{Contrast D} = ((\text{Contrast A} + \text{Contrast B})/2) - \text{Contrast C}$$

All four contrasts were analyzed for each of the 24 outcome variables. Cohen's effect size measure for mean differences (Cohen's d) was also generated for Contrast D. For interpretive purposes, Cohen stated that d values 0.20, 0.50, and 0.80 correspond, respectively, to "small," "moderate," and "large" effects (Cohen, 1988).

Results

Table 1 presents descriptive statistics regarding the sample used in this study. Overall, study participants attended 80.9% of sessions ($M = 6.47$, $SD = 1.68$). Analysis of the treatment fidelity indicates that group leaders covered an average of 92% of the topics described in the treatment manual. There was no statistical difference between the treatment group and wait-list control group on attendance, treatment fidelity, homework compliance, gender, ethnicity, or age. Compliance with homework assignments was very low, with an average of 2.3 homework assignments completed by each participant over the course of the eight sessions.

Although the original research proposal specified that study participants would be randomly assigned to the treatment or wait-list control group, real-world limitations prevented this from being possible. Three participants needed to be placed in the wait-list control group due to the timing of the treatment group sessions. All other participants were randomly assigned. Preliminary analysis required the use of independent samples 2-tailed t-tests. The purpose of this statistical analysis was to compare the two groups at pretreatment to ensure that the groups did not significantly differ on any of the dependent variables at the start of the study. There were no statistically significant differences in age, gender, and ethnicity between the two groups at Time 1 ($t(18) = .452$, $p = .656$; $\chi^2(1, N = 20) = 0.27$, $p = .61$; $\chi^2(1, N = 20) = 0.27$, $p = .61$). Only one dependent variable, the Anger Control composite score on the BASC-2 Teacher Rating Scale, was statistically significant at pretreatment evaluation. At Time 1, teachers rated anger control as significantly poorer in the students assigned to the treatment condition ($M = 64.33$, $SD = 11.54$) compared to those assigned to the wait-list control group ($M = 53.90$, $SD = 7.20$, $t(17) = 2.391$, $p = .029$).

Hypothesis 1: Adolescent Self-Reports (Tables 1 and 2)

Statistical analysis on relevant scales of the BASC-2 self-report of personality revealed no statistical significance between the experimental group and wait-list

TABLE 1   Descriptive Statistics for Adolescent Participants, Parents/Legal Guardians, and Teachers

Variable	Adolescents ($n = 20$)	Parents/legal guardians ($n = 20$)	Teachers ($n=9$)
Age at Tx start			
Mean	13 years, 5 months		
(*SD*)	(0.49 months)		
Gender			
Female	15	19	6
Male	5	1	3
Ethnicity			
Caucasian/White	0	0	6
African American	15	18	2
Hispanic/Latinx	2	2	0
Asian	0	0	1
Biracial/Other	3	0	0

control group on any of the BASC-2 self-report measures. However, Cohen's effect size values were calculated for Contrast D using each of the scales of interest in this study. The effect size for the difference in regarding the Anger Control scale is 0.33. This value can be characterized as a small-to-moderate practical significance using the interpretive standards outlined above. The BASC-2 SRP Emotional Symptoms Index showed a Cohen's effect size of 0.39. This value can be characterized as a small-to-moderate practical significance. The Social Stress scale was found to have a Cohen's *d* value of 0.24, which represented a small practical treatment effect. Analysis of the Relations With Parents scale and the Locus of Control scale revealed no significant treatment effect and a Cohen's effect size value that indicates no practical treatment effects (0.05 and 0.04, respectively).

Statistical analysis revealed a significant treatment effect with regard to the Self-Centeredness subscale as measured by the HIT-Q ($t(31.73) = -2.05$, $p = .05$). The Cohen's effect size value is 0.73 and represents a moderate-to-large treatment effect. Statistically significant treatment effects were not found for the other scales of the HIT-Q, but Cohen's effect sizes were calculated to determine if any practical treatment effects were noted. A moderate-to-large treatment effect was found for the Opposition/Defiance scale on the HIT-Q (Cohen's effect size = 0.72). A

TABLE 2   Overall Adolescent Treatment Effects (*n* = 19)

Variable	*df*	*T*	Cohen's *d*	Effect size
BASC-2 SRP-A Anger Control	31.3	−0.92	0.33	Small-moderate
BASC-2 SRP-A Emotional Symptom Index	30.8	−1.07	0.39	Small-moderate
BASC-2 SRP-A Locus of Control	31.3	−0.12	0.04	
BASC-2 SRP-A Social Stress	30.9	−0.66	0.24	Small
BASC-2 SRP-A Relations With Parents	31.6	0.14	0.05	
HIT-Q Self-Centered	31.7	−2.05*	0.73	Moderate-large
HIT-Q Blaming Others	31.9	−0.67	0.24	Small
HIT-Q Minimizing/Mislabeling	32.2	−0.67	0.24	Small
HIT-Q Opposition/Defiance	31.8	−2.02*	0.72	Moderate-large
HIT-Q Physical Aggression	31.8	−1.06	0.38	Small-moderate
HIT-Q Overall	31.7	−1.19	0.43	Moderate
MSAI Anger Experience	33.7	−1.38	0.48	Moderate

Note. BASC-2 SRP-A = Behavior Assessment Scale for Children, 2nd Edition Self-Report of Personality–Adolescent; HIT-Q = How I Think Questionnaire; MSAI = Multidimensional School Anger Inventory.

*$p < .05$

small-to-moderate treatment effect was noted on the Physical Aggression scale (Cohen's effect size = 0.38). The results of contrast analysis revealed a small treatment effect (Cohen's effect size = 0.24) on the Blaming Others scale and the Minimizing/Mislabeling scale (Cohen's effect size = 0.24). The overall score on the HIT-Q measures an adolescent's overall tendency to endorse cognitive distortions (Barriga et al., 1996). The Cohen's effect size value is 0.43 and represents a moderate treatment effect.

The Anger Experience scale on the MSAI measures an adolescent's experience of anger in a school setting (Smith et al., 1998). Contrast analysis revealed no statistically significant treatment effect with regard to anger experience ($t(33.66) = -1.38$, $p = .18$). However, the Cohen's effect size value is 0.48 and represents a moderate treatment effect.

Hypothesis 2: Parent-Reported Changes (Table 3)

One statistically significant treatment effect was noted on the BASC-2 Parent Rating Scale. A statistically significant treatment effect was found with regard to rule-breaking behavior as measured by the Conduct Problems scales of the BASC-2 Parent Rating Scale ($t(27.24) = -2.11$, $p = .04$). The Cohen's effect size value is 0.81 and represents a large treatment effect. No statistically significant

TABLE 3   Overall Treatment Effects Reported by Parents on the BASC-2 PRS-A (*n* = 19)

Scale	*df*	*T*	Cohen's *d*	Effect size
Aggression	26.7	−0.75	0.29	Small
Conduct Problems	27.2	−2.11*	0.81	Large
Social Skills	31.3	1.5	0.54	Moderate
Anger Control	30.4	−0.45	0.16	
Bullying	27.4	−1.59	0.60	Moderate
Emotional Self-Control	30.0	−0.50	0.19	

Note. BASC-2 PRS-A = Behavior Assessment Scales for Children, 2nd Edition Parent Rating Scale–Adolescent.

treatment effects were found for the other relevant scales of the BASC-2 Parent Rating Scale. However, practical treatment effects were identified by calculating Cohen's effect sizes.

The Cohen's effect size value using the Aggression scale was 0.29 and represents a small treatment effect. The Cohen's effect size value using the Bullying scale was 0.60 and represents a large practical treatment effect. No practical treatment effects were found when calculating effect sizes for the Anger Control and Emotional Self-Control indices (effect sizes = 0.16 and 0.19, respectively). The Cohen's effect size value using the Social Skills scale was 0.54 and represents a moderate treatment effect. Specifically, this result indicates a decline in social skills and an increase in social difficulties as reported by parent raters and represents a change in the undesired direction.

Hypothesis 3: Teacher-Reported Changes (Table 4)

Analysis of the BASC-2 Teacher Rating Scale revealed no statistically significant treatment effects regarding changes in aggression, conduct problems, social skills, bullying, and anger control. Cohen's *d* effect sizes were calculated and revealed a moderate treatment effect on the Anger Control scale (Cohen's effect size = 0.57) and a small treatment effect on the Social Skills scale (Cohen's effect size = 0.20). No practical treatment effects were found on the Aggression, Bullying, and Conduct Problems scales (Cohen's effect sizes = 0.08, 0.15, and 0.12, respectively).

Discussion

This study sought to evaluate preliminary data on the effectiveness of TAME in a middle school setting on Long Island. In addition to teacher reports and parent

TABLE 4   Overall Treatment Effects Reported by Teachers on the BASC-2 TRS-A (*n* = 19)

Scale	*df*	*T*	Cohen's *d*	Effect size
Aggression	32.8	0.22	0.08	
Conduct Problems	32.9	0.34	0.12	
Social Skills	33.1	−0.56	0.20	Small
Anger Control	33.1	−1.64	0.57	Moderate
Bullying	32.8	−0.30	0.11	
Emotional Self-Control	33.2	−0.42	0.15	

Note. BASC-2 TRS-A = Behavior Assessment Scales for Children, 2nd Edition Teacher Rating Scale–Adolescent.

reports, the focus of this study was to evaluate treatment effect via adolescents' self-reports of behavior and cognitive processes.

Participants missed, on average, 1.53 sessions of TAME, which is not uncommon in school-based intervention programs (Mihalic & Irwin, 2003). Reasons for missing sessions included absences from school and out-of-school suspensions. Although study participants actively discussed material in group and enthusiastically conducted role plays and other activities, rates of homework completion were poor. Homework assignments and Hassle Logs are included in the TAME program because self-monitoring has been shown to increase awareness of anger incidents and triggers (Feindler & Baker, 2004). Sukhodolsky et al. (2004) reported that use of homework assignments in anger management programs with children and adolescents contributed to positive therapy outcomes. Homework assignments also allow for rehearsal of new material and encourage generalizability of skills to other environments.

Examination of the Adolescent Treatment Effects (Understanding Hypothesis 1)

At Time 1, except for scores on the BASC-2 Self-Reported Anger Control scale, all other BASC-2 self-reported scale scores used in this study were within normal limits. The same is true for the MSAI Anger Experience scores at Time 1. Participants' ratings were in the borderline and clinical range on the HIT-Q scales. This discrepancy is interesting and perhaps indicates that while participants endorsed elevated amounts of cognitive distortions regarding anger and aggression, they did not report high levels of behaviors. Feindler and Baker (2004) reported that adolescents sometimes underreport anger and aggression in order to appear more socially desirable.

Overall, adolescent self-reports revealed improvements in anger control and emotional functioning following participation in the TAME program. This is consistent with findings by Candelaria et al. (2012) regarding average treatment effects of school-based anger management programs. Anger experience in school was also found to decline following participation in TAME. The greatest impact and largest effect sizes were found for changes in self-reported cognitive distortions regarding oppositional behavior and self-centeredness. Overall, cognitive distortions declined, and a small-to-moderate effect size was found regarding cognitive distortions endorsing the use of physical aggression. It is possible that changes in attitudes and cognitive distortions following the intervention did not yet contribute to substantial changes in behavior. Adolescents may need time to practice skills learned in the TAME program before perceivable behavioral changes can be noted (Bundy et al., 2011).

Examination of Parent-Reported Treatment Effects (Understanding Hypothesis 2)

Results suggest that parents reported a decline in conduct problems following their child's participation in the TAME program. This result was statistically significant for the overall sample and the treatment group from Time 1 to Time 2 and represents a large effect size. The decline in conduct and delinquency issues as reported by parents was greater than the average effect size calculated by Candelaria et al. (2012) in their meta-analysis of 60 school-based anger management studies. Although not statistically significant, a moderate treatment effect was also found with regard to parent-reported improvements in bullying behavior. A small treatment effect was noted for aggression reduction following treatment. The effect sizes for declines in bullying behavior and aggression were consistent with what Candelaria et al. reported. In general, it appears that parents noticed overt behavior change (reduction in conduct problems, bullying, and aggression) in the desired direction following their child's participation in TAME.

Contrary to expectations, parents reported a decline in social proficiency following participation in TAME. While this finding was not statistically significant, it does represent a moderate treatment effect. This unexpected finding is difficult to explain, considering that TAME includes interpersonal effectiveness training; perhaps parents viewed participants' attempts to practice assertiveness skills as negative, possibly because the skills were being misapplied or ineffectively used. Another possibility is that parents anticipated anger management training would encourage their adolescent to be calm and cooperative and found assertive communication undesirable.

Examination of Teacher-Reported Treatment Effects (Understanding Hypothesis 3)

Examination of treatment effects as reported by teachers using the BASC-2 Teacher Rating Scales found a moderate, but nonsignificant, treatment effect with regard to adolescent anger control. This finding indicates that teachers reported a perceivable improvement in the adolescent's tendency to become irritable and maintain self-control in school after participating in the TAME program. Unlike parent-reported treatment effects, teachers reported fewer overall improvements following TAME. This difference may be related to the fact that teachers who volunteered to participate in this study were asked to complete assessment questionnaires on two or three adolescents. Filling out questionnaires on several adolescents may have primed teachers to think about the group of students who participated in the study, rather than the specific adolescent they would otherwise have been asked to evaluate for each questionnaire. Another possible explanation is that parents, having greater contact with the adolescents, had more opportunities to notice change. Given the demands of managing the classroom and presenting material, teachers may not have been as inclined to perceive small changes in the group participants, or salient aggressive events may have had a greater impact on their overall attitude toward that adolescent.

A small treatment effect was also found with regard to improved social skills. This finding is interesting given the fact that parent reports indicate the opposite. Additionally, the differences between self-reports, parent reports, and teacher reports on adolescent behavior following TAME are inconsistent with Candelaria et al. (2012), who found no significant differences between raters in a 60-study meta-analysis.

The fewer changes in adolescent behavior following TAME, as rated by teachers, is especially interesting when one considers that teachers rated participants at the beginning of the study as having elevated rates of aggression, conduct problems, emotional instability, and bullying. In contrast, parent ratings for the same scales were all within normal limits at pretreatment. Overall, it can be stated that teachers viewed study participants as being angrier and more aggressive than other peers at the start of the program and reported little change at post-intervention assessment compared to parent raters. It is difficult to assess which group of raters had more accurate perceptions of the adolescent participants, indicating possible misperception or biased attitude on the part of the parents and/or teachers. Another possibility is that discrepancy between parents and teachers indicated actual differences in behavior at home and at school. If so, each of these perspectives is useful and valuable in understanding the impact of anger management intervention (Sukhodolsky et al., 2004).

Implementation Issues With Clinical Research in Real-World Settings

Mihalic and Irwin (2003) set out to evaluate implementation issues by studying eight violence-prevention programs across 42 U.S. sites over the course of two years. Results indicated that technical assistance, described as regular visitation to the site by the researchers and program experts, helped promote adherence, sustainability, and improved outcomes. One interesting finding from this research suggested that among school and community sites, despite the availability of technical assistance, schools had the greatest difficulty adhering to the program's dosing schedule. The most frequent reason for failure to stick to the treatment schedule was lack of time, given the priority on educational demands. This finding is consistent with the experience of this researcher when implementing TAME in a school setting; scheduling of sessions was dictated by the availability of time in the school day rather than the recommendations set forth by the treatment manual, despite the school administration's desire to participate in the study.

Administrative characteristics within the school or agency were also identified as important factors in successful implementation of violence-prevention programs (Mihalic & Irwin, 2003). This suggests that proper implementation of treatment programs requires more than just administrative approval but necessitates administrative support throughout the process.

Parental education about the TAME program and co-occurring parent training might also have contributed to better treatment outcomes. Additionally, future uses of the TAME program in school settings should be preceded by community education about increasing youth violence and the need for anger management programs for at-risk adolescents.

Among the limitations of the current study was the sample size used ($n = 20$). While only one participant dropped out of the study, nine of the participants had incomplete assessment materials. As a result, a mixed model statistical design was used to evaluate the treatment effect using all sample participants. Sukhodolsky et al. (2004) found that sample sizes in anger management studies with children and adolescents ranged from 10 to 234, but more than 50% of the groups contained 24 or fewer participants. Therefore, the sample size used in this research is consistent with other studies in the field.

Conclusion

Preliminary evidence demonstrates the efficacy of TAME at improving adolescent self-reported anger control and anger experience in school, in addition to changing cognitive distortions regarding aggression, defiance, and self-centeredness. Parents reported improvements in conduct problems and bullying, while teachers reported improved anger control in school. This study validates previously published findings of other CBT approaches to anger-related problems.

Appendix A

In-Session Worksheets

Hassle Log

Name: _____ Date: _____ Time: _____

Where were you?

☐ Home ☐ School ☐ Outside car/bus ☐ Other

What happened?

☐ Teased ☐ Told to do something ☐ Someone started a fight with me
☐ I did something wrong ☐ Someone stole from me ☐ Other

Who was that somebody?

☐ Friend ☐ Sibling ☐ Another student ☐ Parent ☐ Teacher
☐ Another adult ☐ Therapist/counselor ☐ Other

What did you do?

☐ Hit back ☐ Ran away ☐ Yelled ☐ Cried ☐ Ignored
☐ Broke something ☐ Told adult ☐ Was restrained
☐ Walked away calmly ☐ Talked it out ☐ Told friend

How did you handle yourself?

☐ Poorly ☐ Not so well ☐ OK ☐ Good ☐ Great

How angry were you?

☐ Burning mad ☐ Really angry ☐ Moderately angry
☐ Mildly angry ☐ Not angry at all

Notes: _____

From *Teen Anger Management Education: Implementation Guidelines for Counselors,*
© 2021 by E. L. Feindler and G. Sita-Molz. Champaign, IL: Research Press (www.researchpress.com, 800-519-2707).

Pocket Hassle Logs

Name: _____ **Date:** _____ **Time:** _____

Where were you?
☐ Home ☐ School ☐ Outside car/bus ☐ Other

What happened?
☐ Teased ☐ Told to do something ☐ Someone started a fight with me
☐ I did something wrong ☐ Someone stole from me ☐ Other

Who was that somebody?
☐ Friend ☐ Sibling ☐ Another student ☐ Parent ☐ Teacher
☐ Another adult ☐ Therapist/counselor ☐ Other

What did you do?
☐ Hit back ☐ Ran away ☐ Yelled ☐ Cried ☐ Ignored
☐ Broke something ☐ Told adult ☐ Was restrained
☐ Walked away calmly ☐ Talked it out ☐ Told friend

How did you handle yourself?
☐ Poorly ☐ Not so well ☐ OK ☐ Good ☐ Great

How angry were you?
☐ Burning mad ☐ Really angry ☐ Moderately angry
☐ Mildly angry ☐ Not angry at all

Notes: _____

Name: _____ **Date:** _____ **Time:** _____

Where were you?
☐ Home ☐ School ☐ Outside car/bus ☐ Other

What happened?
☐ Teased ☐ Told to do something ☐ Someone started a fight with me
☐ I did something wrong ☐ Someone stole from me ☐ Other

Who was that somebody?
☐ Friend ☐ Sibling ☐ Another student ☐ Parent ☐ Teacher
☐ Another adult ☐ Therapist/counselor ☐ Other

What did you do?
☐ Hit back ☐ Ran away ☐ Yelled ☐ Cried ☐ Ignored
☐ Broke something ☐ Told adult ☐ Was restrained
☐ Walked away calmly ☐ Talked it out ☐ Told friend

How did you handle yourself?
☐ Poorly ☐ Not so well ☐ OK ☐ Good ☐ Great

How angry were you?
☐ Burning mad ☐ Really angry ☐ Moderately angry
☐ Mildly angry ☐ Not angry at all

Notes: _____

Name: _____ **Date:** _____ **Time:** _____

Where were you?
☐ Home ☐ School ☐ Outside car/bus ☐ Other

What happened?
☐ Teased ☐ Told to do something ☐ Someone started a fight with me
☐ I did something wrong ☐ Someone stole from me ☐ Other

Who was that somebody?
☐ Friend ☐ Sibling ☐ Another student ☐ Parent ☐ Teacher
☐ Another adult ☐ Therapist/counselor ☐ Other

What did you do?
☐ Hit back ☐ Ran away ☐ Yelled ☐ Cried ☐ Ignored
☐ Broke something ☐ Told adult ☐ Was restrained
☐ Walked away calmly ☐ Talked it out ☐ Told friend

How did you handle yourself?
☐ Poorly ☐ Not so well ☐ OK ☐ Good ☐ Great

How angry were you?
☐ Burning mad ☐ Really angry ☐ Moderately angry
☐ Mildly angry ☐ Not angry at all

Notes: _____

Name: _____ **Date:** _____ **Time:** _____

Where were you?
☐ Home ☐ School ☐ Outside car/bus ☐ Other

What happened?
☐ Teased ☐ Told to do something ☐ Someone started a fight with me
☐ I did something wrong ☐ Someone stole from me ☐ Other

Who was that somebody?
☐ Friend ☐ Sibling ☐ Another student ☐ Parent ☐ Teacher
☐ Another adult ☐ Therapist/counselor ☐ Other

What did you do?
☐ Hit back ☐ Ran away ☐ Yelled ☐ Cried ☐ Ignored
☐ Broke something ☐ Told adult ☐ Was restrained
☐ Walked away calmly ☐ Talked it out ☐ Told friend

How did you handle yourself?
☐ Poorly ☐ Not so well ☐ OK ☐ Good ☐ Great

How angry were you?
☐ Burning mad ☐ Really angry ☐ Moderately angry
☐ Mildly angry ☐ Not angry at all

Notes: _____

From *Teen Anger Management Education: Implementation Guidelines for Counselors,*
© 2021 by E. L. Feindler and G. Sita-Molz. Champaign, IL: Research Press (www.researchpress.com, 800-519-2707).

Worksheet 2

Group Rules

Use the space underneath to take notes in your own words.

1. Confidentiality

2. Respect yourself, your peers, and the group leader

3. Be present (on time, focused, and ready to listen)

4. Participate in the discussion

5. _____

Goals of the Group

1. Learn new skills to help you control your anger in provocative situations.

2. Increase your personal power by learning skills necessary to communicate needs and desires effectively.

From *Teen Anger Management Education: Implementation Guidelines for Counselors,*
© 2021 by E. L. Feindler and G. Sita-Molz. Champaign, IL: Research Press (www.researchpress.com, 800-519-2707).

Understanding Emotions

What's the difference between emotions and moods?

Emotion is an intense feeling in response to a specific thought, person, or event. Emotions don't last as long (several minutes).

Moods are often made up of different emotions and are not necessarily related to a specific source. Moods often last longer (several hours).

> Every culture gives names to emotions. When people are able to describe and name an emotion, they understand it better and are better able to manage it.

Steps involved with naming emotions and moods:

Step 1: Recognize when you are feeling an emotion.

Step 2: Describe the emotion by considering

- the provoking event
- your interpretation of the event ("Did it happen on purpose or by accident?")
- physiological sensations ("How does my body feel?")
- body language ("How does my face or body posture look?")
- verbal communication of the emotion
- actions or behaviors taken in response to the emotion

Step 3: Name all the different emotions that you are currently feeling or expressing.

From *Teen Anger Management Education: Implementation Guidelines for Counselors,*
© 2021 by E. L. Feindler and G. Sita-Molz. Champaign, IL: Research Press (www.researchpress.com, 800-519-2707).

The Anger Thermometer

Think of the words you use to describe different levels of anger. Where would you put those words on the thermometer?

Physical Cues of Anger

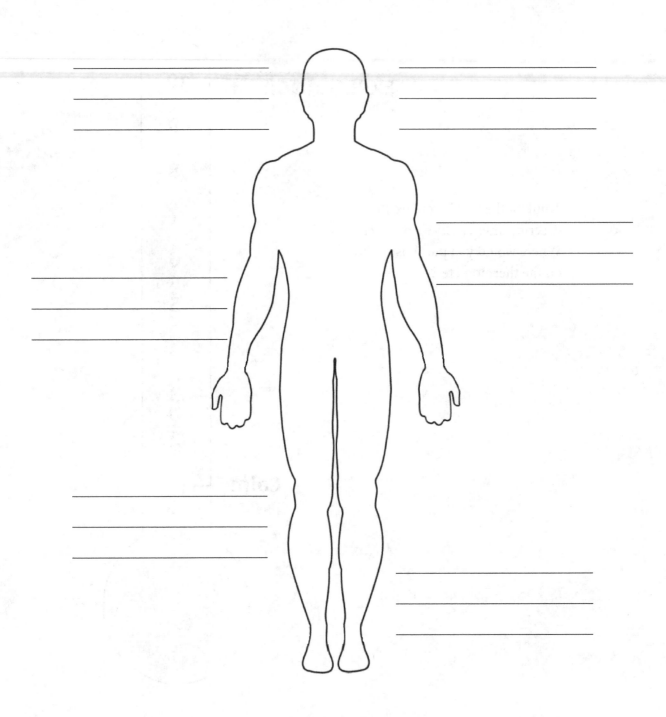

From *Teen Anger Management Education: Implementation Guidelines for Counselors,*
© 2021 by E. L. Feindler and G. Sita-Molz. Champaign, IL: Research Press (www.researchpress.com, 800-519-2707).

Take Three

Taking three slow, deep breaths can help you maintain a controlled response to anger provocations.

Many athletes (e.g., figure skaters, gymnasts, baseball players) visibly use a few deep breaths before attempting some event.

Deep breathing will reduce body tension, refocus attention away from the provoking event, and give you a delay before reacting.

How does a delay before reacting increase your personal power?

From *Teen Anger Management Education: Implementation Guidelines for Counselors,*
© 2021 by E. L. Feindler and G. Sita-Molz. Champaign, IL: Research Press (www.researchpress.com, 800-519-2707).

ABCs of Anger

A **Antecedents**	Direct Triggers	Indirect Triggers
B **Actual Behavior**	Thoughts	Physical Cues
C **Consequences**	Negative	Positive

From *Teen Anger Management Education: Implementation Guidelines for Counselors,*
© 2021 by E. L. Feindler and G. Sita-Molz. Champaign, IL: Research Press (www.researchpress.com, 800-519-2707).

Worksheet 8

Cognitive Appraisal Example

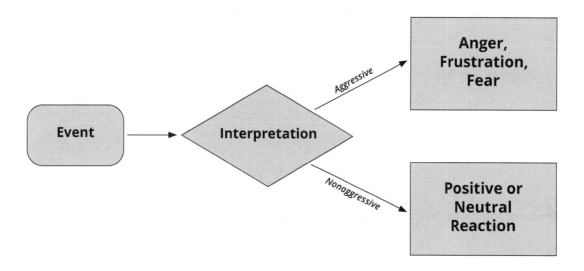

Scenario: *Maria doesn't like Susan or Jenny. Susan gets very angry with Maria for not liking her, but Jenny just gets afraid. Why would they have two different emotions from the same fact that Maria doesn't like them? Susan gets mad because she is thinking how much she has done for Maria and that Maria should therefore appreciate and like her. Meanwhile, Jenny becomes afraid because she thinks that if Maria doesn't like her after all she has done for Maria, then maybe* no one *will like her.*

Aggressive interpretation:

- Thoughts:

- Resulting feelings/reaction:

Nonaggressive interpretation:

- Thoughts:

- Resulting feelings/reaction:

All the Reasons Why

Brainstorm! List all the reasons you can think of why people act in certain ways or do the things they do.

Scenario: *Someone passes you in the hallway and says a derogatory statement as they pass.*

Reasons why:

From *Teen Anger Management Education: Implementation Guidelines for Counselors,*
© 2021 by E. L. Feindler and G. Sita-Molz. Champaign, IL: Research Press (www.researchpress.com, 800-519-2707).

Mindfulness and Rumination

What is **mindfulness?**

- It is a way of paying attention and being more aware of what is happening in the present moment.
- It is something that requires PRACTICE!

ABCs of Mindfulness:

A is for _____—being more conscious of what you are thinking, doing, or feeling in the moment.

B is for _____—to be mindful is to notice your experience without judging it or avoiding it. It means you can just sit with the feeling, sensation, and thought.

C is for _____—when you are more aware of your thoughts, feelings, and actions, you have the power to make choices about how you want to respond or not respond.

Mindfulness is NOT:

_____ *before* _____

Rumination:

_____

"It is like drinking poison and expecting the other person to die."

From *Teen Anger Management Education: Implementation Guidelines for Counselors,*
© 2021 by E. L. Feindler and G. Sita-Molz. Champaign, IL: Research Press (www.researchpress.com, 800-519-2707).

Objectives Effectiveness
Getting what you want

D:

E:

A:

R:

From *Teen Anger Management Education: Implementation Guidelines for Counselors,*
© 2021 by E. L. Feindler and G. Sita-Molz. Champaign, IL: Research Press (www.researchpress.com, 800-519-2707).

Objectives Effectiveness (cont'd)

M:

A:

N:

Relationship Effectiveness
Maintaining good relationships with people you care about

G:

I:

V:

E:

From *Teen Anger Management Education: Implementation Guidelines for Counselors,*
© 2021 by E. L. Feindler and G. Sita-Molz. Champaign, IL: Research Press (www.researchpress.com, 800-519-2707).

Self-Instruction Training

Reminders: Things we say to ourselves to guide our behavior or to get us to remember something.

Give two examples of pressure situations in which reminders are helpful:

1.

2.

What will be your personal reminders for staying calm?

Stop, Press the Pause Button, Kick Back, and Remind.

Thinking Ahead

Consequences of not getting better control of your anger	
Short-term consequences	Long-term consequences

From *Teen Anger Management Education: Implementation Guidelines for Counselors,*
© 2021 by E. L. Feindler and G. Sita-Molz. Champaign, IL: Research Press (www.researchpress.com, 800-519-2707).

Problem Solving
A process used to make a choice between anger control alternatives

- What is the hassle?

- What are my options?

- What is my penalty/consequence?

- What action will I take?

- How did it work?

From *Teen Anger Management Education: Implementation Guidelines for Counselors,*
© 2021 by E. L. Feindler and G. Sita-Molz. Champaign, IL: Research Press (www.researchpress.com, 800-519-2707).

Relational Aggression Example

Relational aggression: the kind of aggression that happens in social relationships in the form of betrayal, gossip, exclusion, humiliation, and lies.

Scenario: Regina and Graciela are good friends and are a part of the same group of friends in their seventh-grade class. Everyone agrees that Graciela is one of the prettiest girls in school. Lately Graciela has been getting a lot of attention from Richard, a popular eighth grader. Regina likes Richard and begins spreading rumors about Graciela. Regina tells people that Graciela thinks she's better than everyone else and even claims that there is a sexual relationship between Richard and Graciela.

- What are the facts?

- What might Graciela be feeling in this situation?

- How do you think Regina is feeling?

- Why is Regina behaving this way?

- If Regina and Graciela don't resolve this problem, what might Graciela learn from the experience?

- Talking it out:

  - What would you say?

  - How would you say it?

  - What is the right time?

From *Teen Anger Management Education: Implementation Guidelines for Counselors,*
© 2021 by E. L. Feindler and G. Sita-Molz. Champaign, IL: Research Press (www.researchpress.com, 800-519-2707).

Self-Respect Effectiveness

1. Be fair to yourself and others.

2. Remember your values, and act accordingly.

3. Be truthful.

From *Teen Anger Management Education: Implementation Guidelines for Counselors,*
© 2021 by E. L. Feindler and G. Sita-Molz. Champaign, IL: Research Press (www.researchpress.com, 800-519-2707).

Friendship Inventory

Every friendship has its ups and downs, but it can be difficult to decide when a friendship is worth saving. A **friendship inventory** is a series of questions that you can ask yourself to help clarify difficult situations.

1. What do you need from a friendship? What makes a good friend?

2. What are your responsibilities in the friendship? What are your friend's responsibilities?

3. What would your friend have to do in order for you to decide to end the friendship?

4. What would *you* have to do in order for *your friend* to decide to end the friendship?

5. What are the pros and cons of ending the friendship?

From *Teen Anger Management Education: Implementation Guidelines for Counselors,*
© 2021 by E. L. Feindler and G. Sita-Molz. Champaign, IL: Research Press (www.researchpress.com, 800-519-2707).

Worksheet 19

TAME Skills Review

- Deep Breathing
- Concept of ABCs
  - ➤ Antecedents
    - Triggers
    - Faulty Reminders
  - ➤ Behavior
  - ➤ Consequences
- Mindfulness and Avoiding Rumination
- Assertion Techniques (DEAR MAN, GIVE, etc.)
- Reminders
- Thinking Ahead
- Problem Solving:

  1. What is the problem?

  2. What *can* I do?

  3. What will happen if…?

  4. What *will* I do?

  5. How did it work?

From *Teen Anger Management Education: Implementation Guidelines for Counselors,*
© 2021 by E. L. Feindler and G. Sita-Molz. Champaign, IL: Research Press (www.researchpress.com, 800-519-2707).

Appendix B

Brief In-Session Mindfulness Activities

Brief In-Session Mindfulness Activities

The following are brief mindfulness activities, for children and adolescents, that were developed by the authors of this book and/or that have been adapted from various online sources/websites (Ackerman, 2020; Hahn, 2011; Life of Tai Chi, n.d.). These activities are suggestions of the kinds of brief mindfulness activities that can be used to orient the group at the start of each session. Group leaders may choose to repeat one activity over multiple sessions or choose a different activity each week.

Mindful Breathing

The script below is designed to be read aloud by the group leader.

> *This mindfulness exercise can be done anytime, standing up or sitting down. Find a comfortable position with your feet planted on the floor. The purpose of this exercise is to focus on your breath for just one minute. Start by breathing in and out slowly, and then hold your breath for a count of six once you've inhaled. Then breathe out slowly, letting the breath flow effortlessly out. While you are focused on your breath, your mind may naturally try to wander. Simply notice these thoughts, let them be for what they are, and return to focusing on your breath. Feel your breath with your senses as it enters your body and fills you with life, and then "watch" it work its way up and out of your body as the energy dissipates into the universe.*

Discussion question: What was it like to do this exercise? Was it easy or difficult—and why?

Mindful Observation

The script below is designed to be read aloud by the group leader.

Find a comfortable position with your feet planted firmly on the ground. Take a deep breath in, and then slowly let it out. Pick something in the environment to focus on for a minute or two. Don't do anything but focus on this element: Look at it closely and with your full attention. Notice its features as if you are seeing it for the first time. Continue taking deep breaths as you do this.

Now close your eyes and listen to the sounds in your environment. Notice all the different sounds, loud and soft, that are around you. Allow yourself to focus only on what you hear, and listen without judgment.

Inhale deeply, and notice the smells around you. Train your attention on the smell you are noticing. Take another deep breath in, and open your eyes.

Discussion question: Is there anything in your environment that you are noticing now that you didn't think about before doing this exercise?

Touch Point

The script below is designed to be read aloud by the group leader.

This exercise is designed to make us appreciate our lives by slowing the pace down, coming into purer awareness, and resting in the moment for a while.

Think of something that happens every day more than once, something you take for granted—like opening a door, for example. At the very moment you touch the doorknob to open the door, allow yourself to be completely mindful of where you are, how you feel, and what you are doing. Let's take a moment to become more aware of our finger coordinating. Place one hand on the table so only your palm is touching the table. One at a time, tap each of your fingers on the table starting with your pinkie, then ring finger, then middle finger, then forefinger, and now thumb. Continue to do this over and over, each time moving a little bit faster. Notice your hand coordination as you do this. Think about all the different muscles and bones that must work together to produce this smooth movement. All of this happens without you even thinking about it at times. For example, think of how much coordination of your fingers is involved in texting or typing.

Choose a touch point that resonates with you today. Instead of going through the motions on autopilot, stop and stay in the moment for a while—and rest in the awareness of this daily activity.

Discussion question: How might being more mindful in your everyday tasks make you more aware of your feelings?

Noticing in Threes

The script below is designed to be read aloud by the group leader.

Sit comfortably, and take three deep breaths in and out slowly.

Look around and see three things you were not previously aware of… 1, 2, 3.

Listen for three sounds you were not aware of… 1, 2, 3.

Feel for three sensations you were not previously aware of… 1, 2, 3.

Discussion questions: What did you notice? How do you feel in this moment?

Body Scan

The script below is designed to be read aloud by the group leader.

Sit in a comfortable position with your feet on the floor. Take in two slow, deep breaths. Begin by feeling the weight of your body on the chair. Notice the points of contact between that and your body. Each time you breathe out, allow yourself to sink a little deeper into the chair. You may feel the breath going in and out of your nostrils or passing through the back of your throat, or you may feel your chest or belly rising and falling. Be aware of your breath wherever it feels most predominant and comfortable for you. Continue for a moment. When you're ready, move your awareness down to your feet. Notice the sensations. Now expand your awareness to your shins and knees. What do they feel like? If you can't feel any sensation, that's okay. As you breathe in, imagine the breath going down your body and into your legs. As you breathe out, imagine the breath going back up your body and out of your nose. Use this strategy of breathing into and out of each part to which you're paying attention. Expand your awareness to your hips. Focus the weight on your bottom on the chair. Breathe into your lower body. Then, when you're ready, let it go. Move up to the lower torso, the lower abdomen, and the lower back. Notice the movement of the lower abdomen as you breathe in and out. Notice any emotions you feel here. See if you can explore and accept your feelings as they are. Bring your attention to your chest and upper back. Feel your rib cage rising and falling as you breathe in and out. Be mindful of your heart beating if you can. Be grateful that all these vital organs are currently functioning to keep you alive and conscious. Go to both arms together, beginning with the fingertips and moving up to the shoulders. Breathe into and out of each body part before you move to the next one, if that feels helpful. Focus on your neck. Then move your mindful attention to your jaw, noticing if it's clenched. Feel your lips, inside your mouth, your cheeks, your nose, your eyelids and eyes, your temples, your forehead (and checking if it's frowning), the back of your head, and finally the top of your head. Take your time to be with each part of your head in a mindful way. Imagine a space in the top of your head. Get a sense of your whole body. Feel yourself as complete, just as you are. Remember this sense of being is always available to you when you need it.

Discussion questions: How was this activity? Were you able to focus? What emotions did you notice?

Mindful Eating

The script below is designed to be read aloud by the group leader, who should provide each group member with a raisin.

First, let's begin by looking at the raisin: What do you see?

What does it smell like?

How does it feel in your hand? Between your fingers?

Put the raisin in your mouth, but don't eat it yet. Just notice how it feels in your mouth. How does it taste?

When you are ready, slowly begin to chew on the raisin. How does the taste change?

Discussion question: How was this experience of eating different from how you usually eat?

Stop Thinking and Count to 10!

The script below is designed to be read aloud by the group leader.

> *Find a comfortable position, and close your eyes. Focus your attention on slowly counting from 1 to 10. If your concentration wanders, go back to 1 and start again. If you notice yourself starting to think of something else or judging yourself for not staying focused, just notice the thoughts and go back to 1. Let's continue this for a minute.*

Discussion question: What was your experience with this activity?

Marble Roll

Materials: Provide an empty paper towel roll or toilet paper roll for each participant and one marble for the group.

Group participants stand in a line, close together. Each participant holds an empty paper towel roll or toilet paper roll. The participant at the head of the line puts the marble in their paper towel roll and tilts it slightly so that the marble rolls into the roll of the person next to them. The object is to try to move the marble from the first person in the line to the last person without dropping the marble. No catching with hands allowed! If someone drops the marble, they must start over again at the beginning of the line.

Discussion question: What did you have to be mindful of while completing this activity?

Different Positions

The script below is designed to be read aloud by the group leader.

> *Can the "shape" of our body affect our mood, emotions, and ability to act? Let's experiment with assuming a few body positions to find out.*
>
> *Start by standing with your feet apart, arms at your sides, with your palms facing in toward your thighs. Take two deep breaths. When you feel fully present, bring your attention to your hands. Keep your awareness on them as you slowly raise them in front of you, and as you do, turn your palms upward. What subtle changes to your mood or emotions do you notice?*

Go back to your original position: arms at your sides, palms facing your thighs. Settle yourself again. Now round your shoulders forward. Drop your head so your chin is on your chest. How does this positioning make you feel? After a few moments, pull your shoulders back while you raise your head to its normal position. Notice the difference in your mood and outlook?

Let's try another position: While standing, lift your chin so that your head is thrown back. A whole new feeling is present. Return your chin to its familiar position. Feel that?

There are many ways to illustrate the power—sometimes quite subtle—that our body position has on our mood. Try hardening your eyes by tightening the muscles around them and staring hard. After a few moments, let your eyes soften. A very subtle change in your mood takes place.

It's also like that with your chin and lips. Tighten your lips as much as you can. Hold it. Now, let them soften. Feel the difference?

Discussion questions: How did your mood change when you assumed different body positions? How might this information about body positioning be helpful in dealing with strong emotions like anger?

Forgiving Ourselves

The script below is designed to be read aloud by the group leader.

Sit with your eyes closed in a comfortable position. Think about something you have done that you wish hadn't happened the way it did (maybe you regret having done or said something that hurt another person). Take a few moments to consider how your actions impacted the other person and how what you do has an impact on how you feel about yourself. While thinking about this situation, also recognize that it's only human to make mistakes. Maybe you feel some shame. That's also human. Offer yourself compassion, for how you've suffered, by thinking, May I be kind to myself. May I accept myself as I am. *If it feels like you need to stay with this thought, keep giving yourself compassion.*

Now try to understand some factors leading to your mistake. Take a moment to consider if there were any environmental factors impacting you at the time. For instance, were you under a lot of stress? Or were certain aspects of your personality triggered in an irrational way—old buttons pushed? Now see if you can offer yourself forgiveness by thinking, May I (begin to) forgive myself for what I have done and for causing hurt to another person? *If it feels right, decide not to make this same mistake—at least to the best of your ability.*

Discussion questions: How was this experience for you? Were you able to give yourself compassion for your mistakes?

Mindfulness Homework

The script below is designed to be read aloud by the group leader.

Pick an activity you do every day without noticing. Instead of completing this task on autopilot, do it one time while being fully aware of your body and the surroundings. For example, brush your teeth mindfully, and notice all the different sensations (the feel of the brush against your teeth and gums, the taste of the toothpaste, the smell, the sounds as you brush, etc.).

Discussion questions: Do you notice anything differently or more intensely when you observe it mindfully? Where is your mind usually while you engage in this activity? How do you feel afterward?

Appendix C

Caregiver Communication Logs

These logs are adapted from anger management programs implemented by Center for Life Resources: Community Connections of Central Texas (CCCT) in Brownwood, TX.

TAME: Caregiver Weekly Communication Log

Week #1 of 12 lessons

Review of group rules, introduction to TAME workbook, discussion of emotions and their impact on physiology, introduction of Hassle Logs.

What to work on at home

Student: Practice using Deep Breathing technique.

Caregiver: Encourage use of Hassle Logs, give reminder to bring TAME workbook each week.

CAREGIVER COMMUNICATION LOG

Student: _____

Caregiver: Write in the box and return to TAME group leader.

Week #2 of 12 lessons

Introduction of ABCs (Antecedent, actual Behavior, Consequence), identifying triggers and consequences (reactions).

What to work on at home

Student: Complete two ABCs worksheets for events that resulted in anger.

Caregiver: Encourage use of Hassle Logs, give reminder to bring TAME workbook each week.

CAREGIVER COMMUNICATION LOG

Student: _____

Caregiver: Write in the box and return to TAME group leader.

From *Teen Anger Management Education: Implementation Guidelines for Counselors,*
© 2021 by E. L. Feindler and G. Sita-Molz. Champaign, IL: Research Press (www.researchpress.com, 800-519-2707).

TAME: Caregiver Weekly Communication Log

Week #3 of 12 lessons

Interpretation of events: how aggressive and nonaggressive beliefs change our feelings toward a situation.

What to work on at home

Caregiver: Encourage use of Hassle Logs, give reminder to bring TAME workbook each week.

CAREGIVER COMMUNICATION LOG

Student: _____

Caregiver: Write in the box and return to TAME group leader.

```



```

TAME: Caregiver Weekly Communication Log

Week #4 of 12 lessons

Mindfulness: discussion focused on how being more mindful can help us control and manage our emotions better. Instead of ruminating, reappraisal can help us lessen the emotional impact of a situation.

What to work on at home

Student: Continue using Hassle Logs, and practice mindfulness while completing a daily task like brushing teeth or eating a snack.

Caregiver: Encourage use of Hassle Logs, give reminder to bring TAME workbook each week.

CAREGIVER COMMUNICATION LOG

Student: _____

Caregiver: Write in the box and return to TAME group leader.

From *Teen Anger Management Education: Implementation Guidelines for Counselors,*
© 2021 by E. L. Feindler and G. Sita-Molz. Champaign, IL: Research Press (www.researchpress.com, 800-519-2707).

TAME: Caregiver Weekly Communication Log

Week #5 of 12 lessons

Being assertive in relationships: DEAR MAN (Describe, Express, Assert, Reinforce, Mindfulness, Appear confident, Negotiate); other techniques: Broken Record, Fogging.

What to work on at home

Student: Practice assertiveness at least twice, and write down the situation to discuss in the next group.

Caregiver: Encourage use of Hassle Logs, give reminder to bring TAME workbook each week.

CAREGIVER COMMUNICATION LOG

Student: _____

Caregiver: Write in the box and return to TAME group leader.

```



```

TAME: Caregiver Weekly Communication Log

Week #6 of 12 lessons

Techniques for helping to maintain relationships: GIVE (Gentle, Interested, Validate, Easy manner).

What to work on at home

Student: Practice using GIVE techniques with friends or family members.

Caregiver: Encourage use of Hassle Logs, give reminder to bring TAME workbook each week.

CAREGIVER COMMUNICATION LOG

Student: _____

Caregiver: Write in the box and return to TAME group leader.

From *Teen Anger Management Education: Implementation Guidelines for Counselors,*
© 2021 by E. L. Feindler and G. Sita-Molz. Champaign, IL: Research Press (www.researchpress.com, 800-519-2707).

TAME: Caregiver Weekly Communication Log

Week #7 of 12 lessons

Effective ways to use reminders as self-control (e.g., Stop, Press the Pause Button, Kick Back, and Remind)

What to work on at home

Student: Practice using reminders for self-control in at least two situations.

Caregiver: Encourage use of Hassle Logs, give reminder to bring TAME workbook each week.

CAREGIVER COMMUNICATION LOG

Student: _____

Caregiver: Write in the box and return to TAME group leader.

```
┌─────────────────────────────────────────────┐
│                                             │
│                                             │
│                                             │
│                                             │
│                                             │
│                                             │
│                                             │
│                                             │
│                                             │
└─────────────────────────────────────────────┘
```

Week #8 of 12 lessons

Thinking Ahead: discussion of long-term and short-term consequences of aggressive behavior, discussion of negative and positive consequences for achieving a different behavior.

What to work on at home

Student: Implement Thinking Ahead techniques.

Caregiver: Encourage use of Hassle Logs, give reminder to bring TAME workbook each week.

CAREGIVER COMMUNICATION LOG

Student: _____

Caregiver: Write in the box and return to TAME group leader.

From *Teen Anger Management Education: Implementation Guidelines for Counselors,*
© 2021 by E. L. Feindler and G. Sita-Molz. Champaign, IL: Research Press (www.researchpress.com, 800-519-2707).

TAME: Caregiver Weekly Communication Log

Week #9 of 12 lessons

Problem solving training sequence and questions to consider: What is the hassle? What are my options? What is my penalty? What actions will I take? Define *self-evaluation*. Feedback: How did it work?

What to work on at home

Student: Use problem solving sequence.

Caregiver: Encourage use of Hassle Logs, give reminder to bring TAME workbook each week.

CAREGIVER COMMUNICATION LOG

Student: _____

Caregiver: Write in the box and return to TAME group leader.

```




```

From *Teen Anger Management Education: Implementation Guidelines for Counselors,*
© 2021 by E. L. Feindler and G. Sita-Molz. Champaign, IL: Research Press (www.researchpress.com, 800-519-2707).

Week #10 of 12 lessons

Bully prevention and questions to discuss: How does relationship aggression (aggression in social relationships, often in the form of rumors, gossip, exclusion, and betrayal) cause problems in friendships? How would you prepare to "talk it out" with a friend?

What to work on at home

Student: Complete the Friendship Inventory worksheet to establish what values are important to you in friendships.

Caregiver: Encourage use of Hassle Logs, give reminder to bring TAME workbook each week.

CAREGIVER COMMUNICATION LOG

Student: _____

Caregiver: Write in the box and return to TAME group leader.

From *Teen Anger Management Education: Implementation Guidelines for Counselors,*
© 2021 by E. L. Feindler and G. Sita-Molz. Champaign, IL: Research Press (www.researchpress.com, 800-519-2707).

TAME: Caregiver Weekly Communication Log

Week #11 of 12 lessons

Review of anger management skills learned.

What to work on at home

Student: Continue practicing skills learned in group; evaluate behavior, thoughts, and feelings following daily hassles to continue to improve anger management strategies.

Please attend booster/follow-up session.

CAREGIVER COMMUNICATION LOG

Student: _____

Caregiver: Write in the box and return to TAME group leader.

From *Teen Anger Management Education: Implementation Guidelines for Counselors,*
© 2021 by E. L. Feindler and G. Sita-Molz. Champaign, IL: Research Press (www.researchpress.com, 800-519-2707).

Appendix D

Session-by-Session Fidelity Checklists

Teen Anger Management Education

Fidelity Checklist

Facility: _____ Date: _____ TAME Session Number: _____

Length of Session: _____ Number of Youth Attending: _____ Number of Leaders: _____

Session 1: Group Orientation	Circle Y or N
Skills and Techniques	
Leaders introduced themselves	Y N
Leaders discussed confidentiality	Y N
Leaders explained rationale of the program	Y N
Leaders explained the rules of the program	Y N
Group practiced mindfulness exercise	Y N
Leaders introduced emotions	Y N
Leaders explained emotions and moods	Y N
Leaders discussed cultural differences regarding emotions and moods	Y N
Leaders explained the steps to naming emotions	Y N
Leaders introduced anger as main focus of the group	Y N
Leaders introduced the Hassle Log	Y N
Leaders distributed and reviewed concepts in Hassle Log	Y N
Leaders demonstrated how to fill out a Hassle Log	Y N
Leaders discussed the rationale for using Hassle Logs	Y N
Exercises	
Group generated a list of physical cues and other cues noticed when anger builds	Y N
Group generated names for different intensities and variations of anger and rated them	Y N
Group participated in Take Three exercise	Y N
Group generated a list of physiological cues they experience when they feel angry	Y N
Leaders demonstrated how to stop and remember to relax when they notice anger building	Y N
Group demonstrated relaxation techniques by provoking each other	Y N
Group practiced diaphragmatic breathing	Y N
Summary and Homework	
Leaders summarized anger and Hassle Logs	Y N
Leaders assigned homework for next session	Y N

From *Teen Anger Management Education: Implementation Guidelines for Counselors,*
© 2021 by E. L. Feindler and G. Sita-Molz. Champaign, IL: Research Press (www.researchpress.com, 800-519-2707).

Teen Anger Management Education

Fidelity Checklist

Facility: _____ Date: _____ TAME Session Number: _____

Length of Session: _____ Number of Youth Attending: _____ Number of Leaders: _____

Session 2: Self-Assessment of Anger and the ABCs of Behavior	Circle Y or N
Review	
Leaders reviewed Hassle Logs	Y N
Leaders explained reason for homework assignments to students who did not comply	Y N
Leaders reviewed brief relaxation techniques and asked if students had difficulty practicing them	Y N
Group practiced mindfulness activity	Y N
Skills and Techniques	
Leaders handed out ABCs worksheet	Y N
Leaders discussed overt activating events	Y N
Leaders discussed covert activating events	Y N
Leaders introduced Antecedents as "A" in ABC chain	Y N
Leaders defined direct triggers	Y N
Leaders defined indirect triggers	Y N
Leaders involved youth in discussion of triggers	Y N
Leaders introduced Behavior as "B" in ABC chain	Y N
Leaders discussed negative statements to self	Y N
Leaders discussed physiological cues	Y N
Leaders involved youth in discussion of cognitive and physiological cues	Y N
Leaders introduced Consequences as "C" in ABC chain	Y N
Leaders elicited examples of positive and negative consequences of temper loss	Y N
Exercises	
Group participated in Trigger Finger exercise	Y N
Leaders demonstrated how direct and indirect triggers can heighten a conflict	Y N
Leaders asked students to role-play provoking each other	Y N
Group participated in Going to the Head exercise	Y N
Group generated a list of positive and negative consequences	Y N
Leaders demonstrated role play of provocative event using ABCs	Y N
Group demonstrated role play of provocative event using ABCs	Y N
Summary and Homework	
Leaders summarized ABCs	Y N
Leaders assigned homework for next session	Y N

From *Teen Anger Management Education: Implementation Guidelines for Counselors,*
© 2021 by E. L. Feindler and G. Sita-Molz. Champaign, IL: Research Press (www.researchpress.com, 800-519-2707).

Teen Anger Management Education

Fidelity Checklist

Facility: _____ Date: _____ TAME Session Number: _____

Length of Session: _____ Number of Youth Attending: _____ Number of Leaders: _____

Session 3: Refuting Aggressive Beliefs	Circle Y or N
Review	
Leaders reviewed Hassle Logs	Y N
Leaders discussed anger-provoking scenarios	Y N
Leaders reviewed aggressive beliefs and asked if students had difficulty recognizing them	Y N
Group practiced mindfulness activity	Y N
Skills and Techniques	
Leaders introduced the interpretation of events	Y N
Leaders discussed the relationship between events and emotions	Y N
Leaders introduced refuting aggressive beliefs	Y N
Leaders discussed the role beliefs play in leading to thoughts	Y N
Leaders defined aggressive beliefs	Y N
Leaders defined nonaggressive beliefs	Y N
Leaders elicited examples of aggressive and nonaggressive beliefs	Y N
Leaders discussed the benefit of interpreting situations nonaggressively	Y N
Leaders involved youth in discussion of interpreting situations nonaggressively	Y N
Exercises	
Group participated in All the Reasons Why exercise	Y N
Group generated a list of nonaggressive explanations	Y N
Group discussed the plausibility of their nonaggressive explanations	Y N
Summary and Homework	
Leaders summarized differences between aggressive and nonaggressive beliefs/ interpretations	Y N
Leaders assigned homework for next session	Y N

Teen Anger Management Education

Fidelity Checklist

Facility: _____ Date: _____ TAME Session Number: _____

Length of Session: _____ Number of Youth Attending: _____ Number of Leaders: _____

Session 4: Mindfulness and Rumination	Circle Y or N
Review	
Leaders reviewed Hassle Logs	Y N
Leaders reviewed refuting aggressive beliefs	Y N
Group practiced mindfulness activity	Y N
Skills and Techniques	
Leaders introduced mindfulness	Y N
Leaders discussed ABCs of mindfulness	Y N
Leaders explained what mindfulness is not	Y N
Leaders introduced concept of rumination	Y N
Leaders contrasted rumination and reappraisal	Y N
Exercises	
Group discussed Emily and Joe scenario	Y N
Group reflected on Ice Cube mindfulness activity	Y N
Summary and Homework	
Leaders reviewed definition of mindfulness	Y N
Leaders described pitfalls of rumination	Y N
Leaders assigned homework for next session	Y N

From *Teen Anger Management Education: Implementation Guidelines for Counselors,*
© 2021 by E. L. Feindler and G. Sita-Molz. Champaign, IL: Research Press (www.researchpress.com, 800-519-2707).

Teen Anger Management Education

Fidelity Checklist

Facility: _____ Date: _____ TAME Session Number: _____

Length of Session: _____ Number of Youth Attending: _____ Number of Leaders: _____

Session 5: Assertiveness Techniques	Circle Y or N
Review	
Leaders reviewed Hassle Logs	Y N
Leaders reviewed aggressive and nonaggressive beliefs and asked if students had difficulty distinguishing them	Y N
Group practiced mindfulness activity	Y N
Skills and Techniques	
Leaders introduced objectives effectiveness	Y N
Leaders explained how to be effective in relationships	Y N
Leaders introduced skills to enhance objectives effectiveness	Y N
Leaders explained "Describe"	Y N
Leaders explained "Express"	Y N
Leaders explained "Assert"	Y N
Leaders explained "Reinforce"	Y N
Leaders explained "Mindful"	Y N
Leaders explained "Appear confident"	Y N
Leaders explained "Negotiate"	Y N
Leaders explained other techniques for achieving objectives	Y N
Exercises	
Group participated in DEAR MAN exercises	Y N
Summary and Homework	
Leaders summarized differences between assertive versus withdrawal or aggressive responses	Y N
Leaders assigned homework for next session	Y N

Teen Anger Management Education

Fidelity Checklist

Facility: _____ **Date:** _____ **TAME Session Number:** _____

Length of Session: _____ **Number of Youth Attending:** _____ **Number of Leaders:** _____

Session 6: Relationship-Building Techniques	Circle Y or N
Review	
Leaders reviewed Hassle Logs	Y N
Leaders asked for examples of practicing assertiveness	Y N
Group practiced mindfulness activity	Y N
Skills and Techniques	
Leaders introduced relationship effectiveness	Y N
Leaders introduced relationship effectiveness skills	Y N
Leaders explained "Gentle"	Y N
Leaders explained "Interested"	Y N
Leaders explained "Validate"	Y N
Leaders explained "Easy manner"	Y N
Exercises	
Group participated in GIVE role plays	Y N
Summary and Homework	
Leaders discussed importance of maintaining connections with others	Y N
Leaders assigned homework for next session	Y N

From *Teen Anger Management Education: Implementation Guidelines for Counselors,*
© 2021 by E. L. Feindler and G. Sita-Molz. Champaign, IL: Research Press (www.researchpress.com, 800-519-2707).

Teen Anger Management Education

Fidelity Checklist

Facility: _____ Date: _____ TAME Session Number: _____

Length of Session: _____ Number of Youth Attending: _____ Number of Leaders: _____

Session 7: Self-Instruction Training	Circle Y or N
Review	
Leaders reviewed Hassle Logs	Y N
Leaders reviewed relationship techniques and asked if students had practiced them	Y N
Group practiced mindfulness activity	Y N
Skills and Techniques	
Leaders introduced self-instruction training	Y N
Leaders defined reminders	Y N
Leaders provided examples of how reminders can be used	Y N
Leaders explained how to implement reminders	Y N
Leaders explained how reminders can be helpful	Y N
Leaders explained the difference between overt and covert reminders	Y N
Leaders role-played overt reminders	Y N
Leaders role-played covert reminders	Y N
Leaders explained the rationale for using covert reminders	Y N
Leaders explained why timing of reminders is critical	Y N
Leaders discussed, with group, situations in which they would not ignore a direct provocation	Y N
Exercises	
Group generated a list of reminders to utilize	Y N
Group participated in It's Hot in the Middle exercise	Y N
Summary and Homework	
Leaders summarized the concept of reminders and the effective use of reminders	Y N
Leaders assigned homework for next session	Y N

From *Teen Anger Management Education: Implementation Guidelines for Counselors,*
© 2021 by E. L. Feindler and G. Sita-Molz. Champaign, IL: Research Press (www.researchpress.com, 800-519-2707).

Teen Anger Management Education

Fidelity Checklist

Facility: _____ Date: _____ TAME Session Number: _____

Length of Session: _____ Number of Youth Attending: _____ Number of Leaders: _____

Session 8: Thinking Ahead	Circle Y or N
Review	
Leaders reviewed Hassle Logs	Y N
Leaders asked group to give each other feedback on how hassles were managed	Y N
Leaders reviewed overt and covert reminders and asked if students had difficulty using them	Y N
Leaders briefly reviewed content from prior sessions (deep breathing, ABCs, assertion techniques, etc.)	Y N
Group practiced mindfulness activity	Y N
Skills and Techniques	
Leaders introduced Thinking Ahead	Y N
Leaders defined Thinking Ahead	Y N
Leaders explained using future negative consequences as reminders to prevent aggressive behaviors	Y N
Leaders defined covert and overt consequences of aggressive behavior	Y N
Leaders explained thinking before acting	Y N
Exercises	
Group generated a list of covert and overt, short- and long-term, internal and external consequences for aggressive behavior	Y N
Group participated in provocation exercise to practice Thinking Ahead	Y N
Group participated in role play using an event from their Hassle Logs	Y N
Summary and Homework	
Leaders summarized the concept of Thinking Ahead by identifying negative consequences	Y N
Leaders assigned homework for next session	Y N

From *Teen Anger Management Education: Implementation Guidelines for Counselors,*
© 2021 by E. L. Feindler and G. Sita-Molz. Champaign, IL: Research Press (www.researchpress.com, 800-519-2707).

Teen Anger Management Education

Fidelity Checklist

Facility: _____ Date: _____ TAME Session Number: _____

Length of Session: _____ Number of Youth Attending: _____ Number of Leaders: _____

Session 9: Problem Solving Training	Circle Y or N
Review	
Leaders reviewed Hassle Logs	Y N
Leaders reviewed Thinking Ahead and asked if students had difficulty doing so	Y N
Group practiced mindfulness activity	Y N
Skills and Techniques	
Leaders introduced problem solving training	Y N
Leaders explained Step 1: problem definition	Y N
Leaders explained Step 2: generation of alternative solutions	Y N
Leaders explained Step 3: consequence evaluation	Y N
Leaders explained Step 4: choosing a solution	Y N
Leaders explained Step 5: self-evaluation	Y N
Leaders explained Step 6: feedback	Y N
Exercises	
Group participated in Where There's a Will, There's a Way exercise	Y N
Group demonstrated problem solving techniques using an example from their Hassle Logs	Y N
Summary and Homework	
Leaders summarized the problem solving sequence	Y N
Leaders assigned homework for next session	Y N

From *Teen Anger Management Education: Implementation Guidelines for Counselors,*
© 2021 by E. L. Feindler and G. Sita-Molz. Champaign, IL: Research Press (www.researchpress.com, 800-519-2707).

Teen Anger Management Education

Fidelity Checklist

Facility: _____ Date: _____ TAME Session Number: _____

Length of Session: _____ Number of Youth Attending: _____ Number of Leaders: _____

Session 10: Bullying Prevention	Circle Y or N
Review	
Leaders reviewed Hassle Logs	Y N
Leaders reviewed problem solving techniques and asked if students had difficulty using them	Y N
Group practiced mindfulness activity	Y N
Skills and Techniques	
Leaders defined relational aggression	Y N
Leaders discussed positive and negative aspects of friendships	Y N
Leaders explained good/friendly teasing	Y N
Leaders explained bad/unfriendly teasing	Y N
Leaders explained the benefits and fears of discussing difficult topics with friends	Y N
Leaders explained the benefits and challenges of apologizing	Y N
Leaders discussed methods of apologizing	Y N
Leaders explained the power of words	Y N
Leaders discussed the power of specific words	Y N
Leaders explained self-respect effectiveness	Y N
Exercises	
Group participated in Rumors exercise	Y N
Group participated in Talking It Out exercise	Y N
Group generated a list of ideas for confronting Regina	Y N
Group role-played confronting Regina	Y N
Group role-played apologizing to Graciela	Y N
Summary and Homework	
Leaders summarized bullying prevention skills	Y N
Leaders assigned homework for next session	Y N

From *Teen Anger Management Education: Implementation Guidelines for Counselors*,
© 2021 by E. L. Feindler and G. Sita-Molz. Champaign, IL: Research Press (www.researchpress.com, 800-519-2707).

References

Ackerman, C.E. (2020, January 10). *22 mindfulness exercises, techniques & activities for adults.* Positive Psychology. https://positivepsychology.com/mindfulness-exercises-techniques-activities/

American Psychiatric Association. (2000). *Diagnostic and statistical manual of mental disorders* (4th ed., text rev.).

American Psychiatric Association. (2013). *Diagnostic and statistical manual of mental disorders* (5th ed.). https://doi.org/10.1176/appi.books.9780890425596

Andreu, J.M., Peña, M.E., & Ramírez, J.M. (2009). Cuestionario de Agresión Reactiva y Proactiva: Un instrumento de medida de la agresión en adolescentes [Reactive and Proactive Aggression Questionnaire: An instrument for measuring aggression in adolescents]. *Revista de Psicopatología y Psicología Clínica, 14*(1), 37–49. https://doi.org/10.5944/rppc.vol.14.num.1.2009.4065

Apsche, J.A., Bass, C.K., & DiMeo, L. (2011). Mode Deactivation Therapy (MDT) comprehensive meta-analysis. *The International Journal of Behavioral Consultation and Therapy, 7*(1), 46–53. https://doi.org/10.1037/h0100926

Bagby, R.M., Taylor, G.J., & Ryan, D. (1986). Toronto Alexithymia Scale: Relationship with personality and psychopathology measures. *Psychotherapy and Psychosomatics, 45*(4), 207–215. https://doi.org/10.1159/000287950

Bariola, E., Hughes, E.K., & Gullone, E. (2012). Relationships between parent and child emotion regulation strategy use: A brief report. *Journal of Child and Family Studies, 21*(3), 443–448. https://doi.org/10.1007/s10826-011-9497-5

Barriga, A.Q., & Gibbs, J.C. (1996). Measuring cognitive distortion in antisocial youth: Development and preliminary validation of the "How I Think" Questionnaire. *Aggressive Behavior, 22*(5), 333–343. https://doi.org/10.1002/(SICI)1098-2337(1996)22:5<333::AID-AB2>3.0.CO;2-K

Barriga, A. Q., Gibbs, J. C., Potter, G., & Liau, A. K. (2001). *How I Think (HIT) Questionnaire: Manual.* Research Press.

Barry, C. T., Grafeman, S. J., Adler, K. K., & Pickard, J. D. (2007). The relations among narcissism, self-esteem, and delinquency in a sample of at-risk adolescents. *Journal of Adolescence, 30*(6), 933–942. https://doi.org/10.1016/j.adolescence.2006.12.003

Bayles, C., Blossom, P., & Apsche, J. (2014). A brief review and update of mode deactivation therapy. *International Journal of Behavioral Consultation and Therapy, 9*(1), 46–48. https://doi.org/10.1037/h0101016

Beck, J. S., Beck, A. T., & Jolly, J. (2001). *Beck Youth Inventories of Emotional and Social Impairment: Manual.* The Psychological Corporation.

Berking, M., & Lukas, C. A. (2015). The Affect Regulation Training (ART): A transdiagnostic approach to the prevention and treatment of mental disorders. *Current Opinion in Psychology, 3*, 64–69. https://doi.org/10.1016/J.COPSYC.2015.02.002

Berking, M., Orth, U., Wupperman, P., Meier, L. L., & Caspar, F. (2008). Prospective effects of emotion-regulation skills on emotional adjustment. *Journal of Counseling Psychology, 55*(4), 485–494. https://doi.org/10.1037/a0013589

Berking, M., Wupperman, P., Reichardt, A., Pejic, T., Dippel, A., & Znoj, H. (2008). Emotion-regulation skills as a treatment target in psychotherapy. *Behaviour Research and Therapy, 46*(11), 1230–1237. https://doi.org/10.1016/j.brat.2008.08.005

Berking, M., & Znoj, H. (2008). Entwicklung und validierung eines fragebogens zur standardisierten selbsteinschätzung emotionaler kompetenzen [Development and validation of a self-report measure for the assessment of emotion-regulation skills]. *Zeitschrift für Psychiatrie, Psychologie und Psychotherapie, 56*(2), 141–153. https://doi.org/10.1024/1661-4747.56.2.141

Betts, J. K., Gullone, E., & Allen, J. S. (2009). An examination of emotion regulation, temperament, and parenting style as potential predictors of adolescent depression risk status: A correlational study. *British Journal of Developmental Psychology, 27*(2), 473–485. https://doi.org/10.1348/026151008X314900

Bögels, S., Hoogstad, B., van Dun, L., de Schutter, S., & Restifo, K. (2008). Mindfulness training for adolescents with externalizing disorders and their parents. *Behavioural and Cognitive Psychotherapy, 36*(2), 193–209. https://doi.org/10.1017/S1352465808004190

Boswell, J. F. (2016). Recognizing anger in clinical research and practice. *Clinical Psychology: Science and Practice, 23*(1), 86–89. https://doi.org/10.1111/cpsp.12137

Boudreaux, D. J., Dahlen, E. R., Madson, M. B., & Bullock-Yowell, E. (2014). Attitudes Toward Anger Management Scale: Development and initial validation. *Measurement and Evaluation in Counseling and Development, 47*(1), 14–26. https://doi.org/10.1177/0748175613497039

Brown, K., Atkins, M. S., Osborne, M. L., & Milnamow, M. (1996). A revised teacher rating scale for reactive and proactive aggression. *Journal of Abnormal Child Psychology*, *24*(4), 473–480. https://doi.org/10.1007/BF01441569

Brown, K. W., & Ryan, R. M. (2003). The benefits of being present: Mindfulness and its role in psychological well-being. *Journal of Personality and Social Psychology*, *84*(4), 822–848. https://doi.org/10.1037/0022-3514.84.4.822

Brown, K. W., West, A. M., Loverich, T. M., & Biegel, G. M. (2011). Assessing adolescent mindfulness: Validation of an adapted Mindful Attention Awareness Scale in adolescent normative and psychiatric populations. *Psychological Assessment*, *23*(4), 1023–1033. https://doi.org/10.1037/a0021338

Bundy, A., McWhirter, P. T., & McWhirter, J. J. (2011). Anger and violence prevention: Enhancing treatment effects through booster sessions. *Education and Treatment of Children*, *34*(1), 1–14. https://doi.org/10.1353/etc.2011.0001

Burney, D. M., & Kromrey, J. (2001). Initial development and score validation of the Adolescent Anger Rating Scale. *Educational and Psychological Measurement*, *61*(3), 446–460. https://doi.org/10.1177/00131640121971310

Burt, I., Patel, S. H., & Lewis, S. V. (2012). Anger management leadership groups: A creative intervention for increasing relational and social competencies with aggressive youth. *Journal of Creativity in Mental Health*, *7*(3), 249–261. https://doi.org/10.1080/15401383.2012.710168

Buss, A. H., & Warren, W. L. (2000). *Aggression Questionnaire (AQ): Manual.* Western Psychological Services.

Candelaria, A. M., Fedewa, A. L., & Ahn, S. (2012). The effects of anger management on children's social and emotional outcomes: A meta-analysis. *School Psychology International*, *33*(6), 596–614. https://doi.org/10.1177/0143034312454360

Capaldi, D. M., & Rothbart, M. K. (1992). Development and validation of an early adolescent temperament measure. *The Journal of Early Adolescence*, *12*(2), 153–173. https://doi.org/10.1177/0272431692012002002

Cavlazoglu, B., Erdogan, N., Paine, T., & Jones, M. (2013). Test review: Anger Regulation and Expression Scale. *Journal of Psychoeducational Assessment*, *31*(1), 84–88. https://doi.org/10.1177/0734282912447762

Champion, K. M. (1997). *Bullying in middle school: Exploring the individual and interpersonal characteristics of the victim* [Unpublished doctoral dissertation]. University of Kansas, Lawrence.

Checa, P., Rodríguez-Bailón, R., & Rueda, M. (2008). Neurocognitive and temperamental systems of self-regulation and early adolescents' social and academic outcomes. *Mind, Brain, and Education*, *2*(4), 177–187. https://doi.org/10.1111/j.1751-228X.2008.00052.x

Ciucci, E., Baroncelli, A., Franchi, M., Golmaryami, F. N., & Frick, P. J. (2014). The association between callous-unemotional traits and behavioral and academic adjustment in children: Further validation of the Inventory of Callous-Unemotional Traits. *Journal of Psychopathology and Behavioral Assessment, 36*(2), 189–200. https://doi.org/10.1007/s10862-013-9384-z

Cliffordson, C. (2001). Parents' judgments and students' self-judgments of empathy: The structure of empathy and agreement of judgments based on the interpersonal reactivity index (IRI). *European Journal of Psychological Assessment, 17*(1), 36–47. https://doi.org/10.1027//1015-5759.17.1.36

Coatsworth, J. D., Duncan, L. G., Greenberg, M. T., & Nix, R. R. L. (2010). Changing parent's mindfulness, child management skills and relationship quality with their youth: Results from a randomized pilot intervention trial. *Journal of Child and Family Studies, 19*(2), 203–217. https://doi.org/10.1007/s10826-009-9304-8

Cohen, J. (1988). *Statistical power analysis for the behavioral sciences* (2nd ed.). Lawrence Erlbaum Associates.

Conners, C. K. (1969). A teacher rating scale for use in drug studies with children. *American Journal of Psychiatry, 126*(6), 884–888. https://doi.org/10.1176/ajp.126.6.884

Crapanzano, A. M., Frick, P. J., & Terranova, A. M. (2010). Patterns of physical and relational aggression in a school-based sample of boys and girls. *Journal of Abnormal Child Psychology, 38*(4), 433–445. https://doi.org/10.1007/s10802-009-9376-3

Dadds, M. R., Cauchi, A. J., Wimalaweera, S., Hawes, D. J., & Brennan, J. (2012). Outcomes, moderators, and mediators of empathic-emotion recognition training for complex conduct problems in childhood. *Psychiatry Research, 199*(3), 201–207. https://doi.org/10.1016/j.psychres.2012.04.033

Davis, M. H. (1983). Measuring individual differences in empathy: Evidence for a multidimensional approach. *Journal of Personality and Social Psychology, 44*(1), 113–126. https://doi.org/10.1037/0022-3514.44.1.113

Davis, M. H., & Franzoi, S. L. (1991). Stability and change in adolescent self-consciousness and empathy. *Journal of Research in Personality, 25*(1), 70–87. https://doi.org/10.1016/0092-6566(91)90006-C

del Barrio, V., Aluja, A., & Spielberger, C. (2004). Anger assessment with the STAXI-CA: Psychometric properties of a new instrument for children and adolescents. *Personality and Individual Differences, 37*(2), 227–244. https://doi.org/10.1016/j.paid.2003.08.014

Denson, T. F., DeWall, C. N., & Finkel, E. J. (2012). Self-control and aggression. *Current Directions in Psychological Science, 21*(1), 20–25. https://doi.org/10.1177/0963721411429451

DiGiuseppe, R., & Tafrate, R. C. (2011). *Anger Regulation and Expression Scale (ARES): Technical manual*. Multi-Health Systems.

Dodge, K. A., & Coie, J. D. (1987). Social-information-processing factors in reactive and proactive aggression in children's peer groups. *Journal of Personality and Social Psychology, 53*(6), 1146–1158. https://doi.org/10.1037/0022-3514.53.6.1146

Ducharme, P., Wharff, E., Hutchinson, E., Kahn, J., Logan, G., & Gonzalez-Heydrich, J. (2012). Videogame assisted emotional regulation training: An ACT with RAGE-Control case illustration. *Clinical Social Work Journal, 40*(1), 75–84. https://doi.org/10.1007/s10615-011-0363-0

Dumas, J. E. (2005). Mindfulness-based parent training: Strategies to lessen the grip of automaticity in families with disruptive children. *Journal of Clinical Child & Adolescent Psychology, 34*(4), 779–791. https://doi.org/10.1207/s15374424jccp3404_20

Duncan, L. G., Coatsworth, J. D., & Greenberg, M. T. (2009). A model of mindful parenting: Implications for parent–child relationships and prevention research. *Clinical Child and Family Psychology Review, 12*(3), 255–270. https://doi.org/10.1007/s10567-009-0046-3

Ehrenreich, J. T., Goldstein, C. R., Wright, L. R., & Barlow, D. H. (2009). Development of a unified protocol for the treatment of emotional disorders in youth. *Child & Family Behavior Therapy, 31*(1), 20–37. https://doi.org/10.1080/07317100802701228

Eifert, G. H., & Forsyth, J. P. (2011). The application of acceptance and commitment therapy to problem anger. *Cognitive and Behavioral Practice, 18*(2), 241–250. https://doi.org/10.1016/j.cbpra.2010.04.004

Ellard, K. K., Fairholme, C. P., Boisseau, C. L., Farchione, T. J., & Barlow, D. H. (2010). Unified protocol for the transdiagnostic treatment of emotional disorders: Protocol development and initial outcome data. *Cognitive and Behavioral Practice, 17*(1), 88–101. https://doi.org/10.1016/j.cbpra.2009.06.002

Ellis, L. K., & Rothbart, M. K. (2001, April). *Revision of the Early Adolescent Temperament Questionnaire* [Poster presentation]. 2001 Biennial Meeting of the Society for Research in Child Development, Minneapolis, MN, United States.

Essau, C. A., Sasagawa, S., & Frick, P. J. (2006). Callous-unemotional traits in a community sample of adolescents. *Assessment, 13*(4), 454–469. https://doi.org/10.1177/1073191106287354

Feindler, E. L., & Baker, K. (2010). Current issues in anger management interventions with youth. In A. P. Goldstein, R. Nensén, B. Daleflod, & M. Kalt (Eds.), *New perspectives on aggression replacement training: Practice, research and application* (pp. 31–50). Wiley.

Feindler, E. L., & Gerber, M. F. (2008). TAME: Teen Anger Management Education. In C. W. LeCroy (Ed.), *Handbook of evidence-based treatment manuals for children and adolescents* (2nd ed., pp. 139–169). Oxford University Press.

Feldman, G., Hayes, A., Kumar, S., Greeson, J., & Laurenceau, J.-P. (2007). Mindfulness and emotion regulation: The development and initial validation of the Cognitive and Affective Mindfulness Scale-Revised (CAMS-R). *Journal of Psychopathology and Behavioral Assessment, 29*(3), 177–190. https://doi.org/10.1007/s10862-006-9035-8

Fernández, M. E. P., Rodríguez, J. M. A., Barriga, A., & Gibbs, J. (2013). Psychometrical properties of the "How I Think" Questionnaire (HIT-Q) in adolescents. *Psicothema, 25*(4), 542–548. https://doi.org/10.7334/psicothema2013.38

Fives, C. J., Kong, G., Fuller, J. R., & DiGiuseppe, R. (2011). Anger, aggression, and irrational beliefs in adolescents. *Cognitive Therapy and Research, 35*(3), 199–208. https://doi.org/10.1007/s10608-009-9293-3

Forbes, D., Alkemade, N., Mitchell, D., Elhai, J. D., McHugh, T., Bates, G., Novaco, R. W., Bryant, R., & Lewis, V. (2014). Utility of the Dimensions of Anger Reactions-5 (DAR-5) Scale as a brief anger measure. *Depression and Anxiety, 31*(2), 166–173. https://doi.org/10.1002/da.22148

Frick, P. J. (2003). *Inventory of Callous-Unemotional Traits* [Unpublished rating scale]. University of New Orleans.

Frick, P. J., Bodin, S. D., & Barry, C. T. (2000). Psychopathic traits and conduct problems in community and clinic-referred samples of children: Further development of the Psychopathy Screening Device. *Psychological Assessment, 12*(4), 382–393.

Frick, P. J., Cornell, A. H., Barry, C. T., Bodin, S. D., & Dane, H. E. (2003). Callous-unemotional traits and conduct problems in the prediction of conduct problem severity, aggression, and self-report of delinquency. *Journal of Abnormal Child Psychology, 31*(4), 457–470. https://doi.org/10.1023/a:1023899703866

Frick, P. J., & Hare, R. D. (2001). *Antisocial Process Screening Device (APSD): Technical manual.* Multi-Health Systems.

Fullan, M. G. (1992). *Successful school improvement: The implementation perspective and beyond.* Open University Press.

Furlong, M. J., Smith, D. C., & Bates, M. P. (2002). Further development of the Multidimensional School Anger Inventory: Construct validation, extension to female adolescents, and preliminary norms. *Journal of Psychoeducational Assessment, 20*(1), 46–65. https://doi.org/10.1177/073428290202000104

Gerhart, J., Holman, K., Seymour, B., Dinges, B., & Ronan, G. F. (2015). Group process as a mechanism of change in the group treatment of anger and aggression.

International Journal of Group Psychotherapy, *65*(2), 180–208. https://doi.org/10.1521/ijgp.2015.65.2.180

Gillanders, D. T., Bolderston, H., Bond, F. W., Dempster, M., Flaxman, P. E., Campbell, L., Kerr, S., Tansey, L., Noel, P., Ferenbach, C., Masley, S., Roach, L., Lloyd, J., May, L., Clarke, S., & Remington, B. (2014). The development and initial validation of the Cognitive Fusion Questionnaire. *Behavior Therapy*, *45*(1), 83–101. https://doi.org/10.1016/j.beth.2013.09.001

Glisson, C., Schoenwald, S. K., Kelleher, K., Landsverk, J., Hoagwood, K. E., Mayberg, S., Green, P., & The Research Network on Youth Mental Health (2008). Therapist turnover and new program sustainability in mental health clinics as a function of organizational culture, climate, and service structure. *Administration and Policy in Mental Health and Mental Health Services Research*, *35*(1–2), 124–133. https://doi.org/10.1007/s10488-007-0152-9

Goldstein, N. E. S., Serico, J. M., Riggs Romaine, C. L., Zelechoski, A. D., Kalbeitzer, R., Kemp, K., & Lane, C. (2013). Development of the juvenile justice anger management treatment for girls. *Cognitive and Behavioral Practice*, *20*(2), 171–188. https://doi.org/10.1016/j.cbpra.2012.06.003

Gratz, K. L., Bardeen, J. R., Levy, R., Dixon-Gordon, K. L., & Tull, M. T. (2015). Mechanisms of change in an emotion regulation group therapy for deliberate self-harm among women with borderline personality disorder. *Behavior Research and Therapy*, *65*, 29–35. https://doi.org/10.1016/j.brat.2014.12.005

Gratz, K. L., & Roemer, L. (2004). Multidimensional assessment of emotion regulation and dysregulation: Development, factor structure, and initial validation of the Difficulties in Emotion Regulation Scale. *Journal of Psychopathology and Behavioral Assessment*, *26*(1), 41–54. https://doi.org/10.1007/s10862-008-9102-4

Gravetter, F. J., & Wallnau, L. B. (2007). *Essentials of statistics for the behavioral sciences*. Wadsworth Publishing.

Greeson, J. M., Webber, D. M., Smoski, M. J., Brantley, J. G., Ekblad, A. G., Suarez, E. C., & Wolever, R. Q. (2011). Changes in spirituality partly explain health-related quality of life outcomes after mindfulness-based stress reduction. *Journal of Behavioral Medicine*, *34*(6), 508–518. https://doi.org/10.1007/s10865-011-9332-x

Gross, J. J. (2002). Emotion regulation: Affective, cognitive, and social consequences. *Psychophysiology*, *39*(3), 281–291. https://doi.org/10.1017/S0048577201393198

Gross, J. J., & John, O. P. (2003). Individual differences in two emotion regulation processes: Implications for affect, relationships, and well-being. *Journal of Personality and Social Psychology*, *85*(2), 348–362. https://doi.org/10.1037/0022-3514.85.2.348

Gullone, E., Hughes, E. K., King, N. J., & Tonge, B. (2010). The normative development of emotion regulation strategy use in children and adolescents: A 2-year follow-up study. *The Journal of Child Psychology and Psychiatry*, *51*(5), 567–574. https://doi.org/10.1111/j.1469-7610.2009.02183.x

Gullone, E., & Taffe, J. (2012). The Emotion Regulation Questionnaire for Children and Adolescents (ERQ-CA): A psychometric evaluation. *Psychological Assessment*, *24*(2), 409–417. https://doi.org/10.1037/a0025777

Hahn, T. N. (2011). *Planting seeds: Practicing mindfulness with children*. Parallax Press.

Herrmann, D. S., & McWhirter, J. J. (2003). Anger & aggression management in young adolescents: An experimental validation of the SCARE program. *Education and Treatment of Children*, *26*(3), 273–302.

Herts, K. L., McLaughlin, K. A., & Hatzenbuehler, M. L. (2012). Emotion dysregulation as a mechanism linking stress exposure to adolescent aggressive behavior. *Journal of Abnormal Child Psychology*, *40*(7), 1111–1122. https://doi.org/10.1007/s10802-012-9629-4

Hofmann, S. G., Carpenter, J. K., & Curtiss, J. (2016). Interpersonal Emotion Regulation Questionnaire (IERQ): Scale development and psychometric characteristics. *Cognitive Therapy and Research*, *40*(3), 341–356. https://doi.org/10.1007/s10608-016-9756-2

Hofmann, S. G., & Kashdan, T. B. (2010). The Affective Style Questionnaire: Development and psychometric properties. *Journal of Psychopathology and Behavioral Assessment*, *32*(2), 255–263. https://doi.org/10.1007/s10862-009-9142-4

Hurrell, K. E., Hudson, J. L., & Schniering, C. A. (2015). Parental reactions to children's negative emotions: Relationships with emotion regulation in children with an anxiety disorder. *Journal of Anxiety Disorders*, *29*, 72–82. https://doi.org/10.1016/j.janxdis.2014.10.008

Ingoglia, S., Lo Coco, A., & Albiero, P. (2016). Development of a Brief Form of the Interpersonal Reactivity Index (B-IRI). *Journal of Personality Assessment*, *98*(5), 461–471. https://doi.org/10.1080/00223891.2016.1149858

Jacobs, G. A., Phelps, M., & Rohrs, B. (1989). Assessment of anger expression in children: The Pediatric Anger Expression Scale. *Personality and Individual Differences*, *10*(1), 59–65. https://doi.org/10.1016/0191-8869(89)90178-5

Katz, L. F., Maliken, A. C., & Stettler, N. M. (2012). Parental meta-emotion philosophy: A review of research and theoretical framework. *Child Development Perspectives*, *6*(4), 417–422. https://doi.org/10.1111/j.1750-8606.2012.00244.x

Kazantzis, N., & Shinkfield, G. (2007). Conceptualizing patient barriers to nonadherence with homework assignments. *Cognitive and Behavioral Practice*, *14*(3), 317–324. https://doi.org/10.1016/j.cbpra.2006.08.003

Keiley, M. K. (2002). The development and implementation of an affect regulation and attachment intervention for incarcerated adolescents and their parents. *The Family Journal, 10*(2), 177–189. https://doi.org/10.1177/1066480702102007

Kerns, C. E., Comer, J. S., & Zeman, J. (2014). A preliminary psychometric evaluation of a parent-report measure of child emotional awareness and expression in a sample of anxious youth. *Cognitive Therapy and Research, 38*(3), 349–357. https://doi.org/10.1007/s10608-014-9596-x

Kimonis, E. R., Fanti, K., Goldweber, A., Marsee, M. A., Frick, P. J., & Cauffman, E. (2014). Callous-unemotional traits in incarcerated adolescents. *Psychological Assessment, 26*(1), 227–237. https://doi.org/10.1037/a0034585

Kimonis, E. R., Frick, P. J., Skeem, J. L., Marsee, M. A., Cruise, K., Munoz, L. C., Aucoin, K. J., & Morris, A. S. (2008). Assessing callous-unemotional traits in adolescent offenders: Validation of the Inventory of Callous-Unemotional Traits. *International Journal of Law and Psychiatry, 31*(3), 241–252. https://doi.org/10.1016/j.ijlp.2008.04.002

Langley, A. K., Nadeem, E., Kataoka, S. H., Stein, B. D., & Jaycox, L. H. (2010). Evidence-based mental health programs in schools: Barriers and facilitators of successful implementation. *School Mental Health, 2*(3), 105–113. https://doi.org/10.1007/s12310-010-9038-1

Lantrip, C., Isquith, P. K., Koven, N. S., Welsh, K., & Roth, R. M. (2016). Executive function and emotion regulation strategy use in adolescents. *Applied Neuropsychology: Child, 5*(1), 50–55. https://doi.org/10.1080/21622965.2014.960567

Leve, L. D., Chamberlain, P., & Kim, H. K. (2015). Risks, outcomes, and evidence-based interventions for girls in the US juvenile justice system. *Clinical Child and Family Psychology Review, 18*(3), 252–279. https://doi.org/10.1007/s10567-015-0186-6

Life of Tai Chi. (n.d.). *Mental boxing.* https://www.taichifuture.com/mental-boxing.html

Linehan, M. M. (1993a). *Diagnosis and treatment of mental disorders. Skills training manual for treating borderline personality disorder.* Guilford Press.

Linehan, M. M. (1993b). *Cognitive-behavioral treatment of borderline personality disorder.* Guilford Press.

Little, T. D., Brauner, J., Jones, S. M., Knock, M. K., & Hawley, P. H. (2004). Rethinking aggression: A typological examination of the functions of aggression. *Merrill-Palmer Quarterly, 49*(3), 343–369. https://doi.org/10.1353/mpq.2003.0014

Little, T. D., Jones, S. M., Henrich, C. C., & Hawley, P. H. (2003). Disentangling the "whys" from the "whats" of aggressive behavior. *International Journal of Behavioral Development, 27*(2), 122–183. https://doi.org/10.1080/01650250244000128

Lochman, J. E., & Wells, K. C. (2002). Contextual social-cognitive mediators and child outcome: A test of the theoretical model in the Coping Power program.

Development and Psychopathology, 14(4), 945–967. https://doi.org/10.1017/S0954579402004157

Lochman, J. E., & Wells, K. C. (2003). Effectiveness of the Coping Power program and of classroom intervention with aggressive children: Outcomes at a 1-year follow-up. *Behavior Therapy, 34*(4), 493–515. https://doi.org/10.1016/S0005-7894(03)80032-1

MacDermott, S. T., Gullone, E., Allen, J. S., King, N. J., & Tonge, B. (2010). The Emotion Regulation Index for Children and Adolescents (ERICA): A psychometric investigation. *Journal of Psychopathology and Behavioral Assessment, 32*(3), 301–314. https://doi.org/10.1007/s10862-009-9154-0

Marsee, M. A., Barry, C. T., Childs, K. K., Frick, P. J., Kimonis, E. R., Centifanti, L. C., Aucoin, K. J., Fassnacht, G. M., Kunimatsu, M. M., & Lau, K. S. L. (2011). Assessing the forms and functions of aggression using self-report: Factor structure and invariance of the Peer Conflict Scale in youths. *Psychological Assessment, 23*(3), 792–804. https://doi.org/10.1037/a0023369

Marsee, M. A., & Frick, P. J. (2007). Exploring the cognitive and emotional correlates to proactive and reactive aggression in a sample of detained girls. *Journal of Abnormal Child Psychology, 35*(6), 969–981. https://doi.org/10.1007/s10802-007-9147-y

Marsee, M. A., Frick, P. J., Barry, C. T., Kimonis, E. R., Muñoz, L. C., & Aucoin, K. J. (2014). Profiles of the forms and functions of self-reported aggression in three adolescent samples. *Development and Psychopathology, 26*(3), 705–720. https://doi.org/10.1017/S0954579414000339

Marsee, M. A., Lau, K. S. L., & Lapré, G. E. (2014). Parent and adolescent report of the forms and functions of aggression: Associations with delinquency, CU traits, and dysregulation. *Child & Youth Care Forum, 43*(1), 27–39. https://doi.org/10.1007/s10566-013-9223-0

Maxwell, J. P., Sukhodolsky, D. G., Chow, C. C. F., & Wong, C. F. C. (2005). Anger rumination in Hong Kong and Great Britain: Validation of the scale and a cross-cultural comparison. *Personality and Individual Differences, 39*(6), 1147–1157. https://doi.org/10.1016/j.paid.2005.03.022

McLaughlin, K. A., Hatzenbuehler, M. L., Mennin, D. S., & Nolen-Hoeksema, S. (2011). Emotion dysregulation and adolescent psychopathology: A prospective study. *Behaviour Research and Therapy, 49*(9), 544–554. https://doi.org/10.1016/j.brat.2011.06.003

McWhirter, P. T., & McWhirter, J. J. (2010). Community and school violence and risk reduction: Empirically supported prevention. *Group Dynamics: Theory, Research, and Practice, 14*(3), 242–256. https://doi.org/10.1037/a0020056

Mezzich, A. C., Tarter, R. E., Giancola, P. R., & Kirisci, L. (2001). The Dysregulation Inventory: A new scale to assess the risk for substance use disorder. *Journal of Child & Adolescent Substance Abuse, 10*(4), 35–43. https://doi.org/10.1300/J029v10n04_04

Mihalic, S. F., & Irwin, K. (2003). Blueprints for violence prevention: From research to real-world settings—factors influencing the successful replication of model programs. *Youth Violence and Juvenile Justice, 1*(4), 307–329. https://doi.org/10.1177/1541204003255841

Miller, A. L., Glinski, J., Woodberry, K. A., Mitchell, A . G., & Indik, J. (2002). Family therapy and dialectical behavior therapy with adolescents: Part I: Proposing a clinical synthesis. *The American Journal of Psychotherapy, 56*(4), 568–584. https://doi.org/10.1176/appi.psychotherapy.2002.56.4.568

Moretti, M. M., Odgers, C., Reppucci, N. D., The Gender and Aggression Project Team, & Catherine, N. L. A. (2011). Serious conduct problems among girls at risk: Translating research into intervention. *International Journal of Child, Youth and Family Studies, 2*(1/2), 142–161. https://doi.org/10.18357/ijcyfs21/220115431

Muñoz, L. C., & Frick, P. J. (2007). The reliability, stability, and predictive utility of the self-report version of the Antisocial Process Screening Device. *Scandinavian Journal of Psychology, 48*(4), 299–312. https://doi.org/10.1111/j.1467-9450.2007.00560.x

Muñoz, L. C., Frick, P. J., Kimonis, E. R., & Aucoin, K. J. (2008). Types of aggression, responsiveness to provocation, and callous-unemotional traits in detained adolescents. *Journal of Abnormal Child Psychology, 36*(1), 15–28. https://doi.org/10.1007/s10802-007-9137-0

Muratori, P., Bertacchi, I., Giuli, C., Lombardi, L., Bonetti, S., Nocentini, A., Manfredi, A., Polidori, L., Ruglioni, L., Milone, A., & Lochman, J. E. (2015). First adaptation of Coping Power program as a classroom-based prevention intervention on aggressive behaviors among elementary school children. *Prevention Science, 16*(3), 432–439. https://doi.org/10.1007/s11121-014-0501-3

Muris, P., & Meesters, C. (2009). Reactive and regulative temperament in youths: Psychometric evaluation of the Early Adolescent Temperament Questionnaire-Revised (EATQ-R). *Journal of Psychopathology and Behavioral Assessment, 31*(1), 7–19. https://doi.org/10.1007/s10862-008-9089-x

Musante, L., Treiber, F. A., Davis, H. C., Waller, J. L., & Thompson, W. O. (1999). Assessment of self-reported anger expression in youth. *Assessment, 6*(3), 225–233. https://doi.org/10.1177/107319119900600303

Mynard, H., & Joseph, S. (2000). Development of the Multidimensional Peer-Victimization Scale. *Aggressive Behavior, 26*(2), 169–178. https://doi.org/10.1002/(SICI)1098-2337(2000)26:2<169::AID-AB3>3.0.CO;2-A

Neuman, A., van Lier, P. A. C., Gratz, K. L., & Koot, H. M. (2010). Multidimensional assessment of emotion regulation difficulties in adolescents using the Difficulties in Emotion Regulation Scale. *Assessment, 17*(1), 138–149. https://doi.org/10.1177/1073191109349579

Norcross, J. C., Krebs, P. M., & Prochaska, J. O. (2011). Stages of change. *Journal of Clinical Psychology, 67*(2), 143–154. https://doi.org/10.1002/jclp.20758

Novaco, R. W. (1975). *Dimensions of anger reactions.* University of California.

Pardini, D. A., Lochman, J. E., & Frick, P. J. (2003). Callous/unemotional traits and social-cognitive processes in adjudicated youths. *Journal of the American Academy of Child and Adolescent Psychiatry, 42*(3), 364–371. https://doi.org/10.1097/00004583-200303000-00018

Penza-Clyve, S., & Zeman, J. (2002). Initial validation of the Emotion Expression Scale for Children (EESC). *Journal of Clinical Child & Adolescent Psychology, 31*(4), 540–547. https://doi.org/10.1207/S15374424JCCP3104_12

Poythress, N. G., Douglas, K. S., Falkenbach, D., Cruise, K., Lee, Z., Murrie, D. C., & Vitacco, M. (2006). Internal consistency reliability of the self-report Antisocial Process Screening Device. *Assessment, 13*(1), 107–113. https://doi.org/10.1177/1073191105284279

Prinstein, M. J., Boergers, J., & Vernberg, E. M. (2001). Overt and relational aggression in adolescents: Social-psychological adjustment of aggressors and victims. *Journal of Clinical Child Psychology, 30*(4), 479–491. https://doi.org/10.1207/S15374424JCCP3004_05

Raine, A., Dodge, K., Loeber, R., Gatzke-Kopp, L., Lynam, D., Reynolds, C., Stouthamer-Loeber, M., & Liu, J. (2006). The Reactive–Proactive Aggression Questionnaire: Differential correlates of reactive and proactive aggression in adolescent boys. *Aggressive Behavior, 32*(2), 159–171. https://doi.org/10.1002/ab.20115

Röll, J., Koglin, U., & Petermann, F. (2012). Emotion regulation and childhood aggression: Longitudinal associations. *Child Psychiatry and Human Development, 43*(6), 909–923. https://doi.org/10.1007/s10578-012-0303-4

Ronan, G. F., Dreer, L. E., Dollard, K. M., & Ronan, D. W. (2004). Violent couples: Coping and communication skills. *Journal of Family Violence, 19*(2), 131–137. https://doi.org/10.1023/B:JOFV.0000019843.26331.cf

Ronan, G. F., Keeney, J., Date, A., & Ronan, D. (1996, November). *Content specificity of communication skill deficits in maritally violent couples* [Conference presentation]. Thirtieth annual meeting of the Association for the Advancement of Behavior Therapy, New York, NY, United States.

Roose, A., Bijttebier, P., Decoene, S., Claes, L., & Frick, P. J. (2010). Assessing the affective features of psychopathy in adolescence: A further validation of the inventory of callous and unemotional traits. *Assessment, 17*(1), 44–57. https://doi.org/10.1177/1073191109344153

Ruzek, J. I., & Rosen, R. C. (2009). Disseminating evidence-based treatments for PTSD in organizational settings: A high priority focus area. *Behaviour Research and Therapy, 47*(11), 980–989. https://doi.org/10.1016/j.brat.2009.07.008

Schoenwald, S. K., Chapman, J. E., Kelleher, K., Hoagwood, K. E., Landsverk, J., Stevens, J., Glisson, C., Rolls-Reutz, J., & The Research Network on Mental Health. (2008). A survey of the infrastructure for children's mental health services: Implications for the implementation of empirically supported treatments (ESTs). *Administration and Policy in Mental Health and Mental Health Services Research, 35*(1–2), 84–97. https://doi.org/10.1007/s10488-007-0147-6

Shetgiri, R., Simon, C. L., Tillitski, J., Wilson, C., & Flores, G. (2015). Why adolescents fight: A qualitative study of youth perspectives on fighting and its prevention. *Academic Pediatrics, 15*(1), 103–110. https://doi.org/10.1016/j.acap.2014.06.020

Shields, A., & Cicchetti, D. (1997). Emotion regulation among school-age children: The development and validation of a new criterion Q-sort scale. *Developmental Psychology, 33*(6), 906–916. https://doi.org/10.1037/0012-1649.33.6.906

Smith, D. C., Furlong, M., Bates, M., & Laughlin, J. D. (1998). Development of the Multidimensional School Anger Inventory for males. *Psychology in the Schools, 35*(1), 1–15. https://doi.org/10.1002/(SICI)1520-6807(199801)35:1<1::AID-PITS1>3.0.CO;2-U

Sportsman, E. L., Carlson, J. S., & Guthrie, K. M. (2010). Lesson learned from leading an anger management group using the "Seeing Red" curriculum within an elementary school. *Journal of Applied School Psychology, 26*(4), 339–350. https://doi.org/10.1080/15377903.2010.518823

Sukhodolsky, D. G., Golub, A., & Cromwell, E. N. (2001). Development and validation of the Anger Rumination Scale. *Personality and Individual Differences, 31*(5), 689–700. https://doi.org/10.1016/S0191-8869(00)00171-9

Sukhodolsky, D., Kassinove, H., & Gorman, B. S. (2004). Cognitive-behavioral therapy for anger in children and adolescents: A meta-analysis. *Aggression and Violent Behavior, 9*(3), 247–269. https://doi.org/10.1016/j.avb.2003.08.005

Suveg, C., Sood, E., Comer, J. S., & Kendall, P. C. (2009). Changes in emotion regulation following cognitive-behavioral therapy for anxious youth. *Journal of Clinical Child & Adolescent Psychology, 38*(3), 390–401. https://doi.org/10.1080/15374410902851721

Tackett, J. L., & Ostrov, J. M. (2010). Measuring relational aggression in middle childhood in a multi-informant multi-method study. *Journal of Psychopathology and Behavioral Assessment, 32*(4), 490–500. https://doi.org/10.1007/s10862-010-9184-7

Tangney, J. P., Wagner, P. E., Gavlas, J., & Gramzow, R. (1991). *The Anger Response Inventory for Adolescents (ARI-A)*. George Mason University.

Törestad, B. (1990). What is anger provoking? A psychophysical study of perceived causes of anger. *Aggressive Behavior, 16*(1), 9–26. https://doi.org/10.1002/1098-2337(1990)16:1%3C9::AID-AB2480160103%3E3.0.CO;2-R

Trosper, S. E., & Ehrenreich-May, J. (2011). The relationship between trait, expressive, and familial correlates of emotion regulation in a clinical sample of anxious youth. *Journal of Emotional and Behavioral Disorders, 19*(2), 117–128. https://doi.org/10.1177/1063426609353763

Vernberg, E. M., Fonagy, P., & Twemlow, S. (2000). *Preliminary report of the Topeka Peaceful Schools Project*. Menninger Clinic.

Verschuere, B., Candel, I., Van Reenan, L., & Korebrits, A. (2012). Validity of the Modified Child Psychopathology Scale for juvenile justice center residents. *Journal of Psychopathology and Behavioral Assessment, 34*(2), 244–252. https://doi.org/10.1007/s10862-011-9272-3

Vitaro, F., Brendgen, M., & Tremblay, R. E. (2002). Reactively and proactively aggressive children: Antecedent and subsequent characteristics. *The Journal of Child Psychology and Psychiatry, 43*(4), 495–505. https://doi.org/10.1111/1469-7610.00040

Voulgaridou, I., & Kokkinos, C. M. (2015). Relational aggression in adolescents: A review of theoretical and empirical research. *Aggression and Violent Behavior, 23*, 87–97. https://doi.org/10.1016/j.avb.2015.05.006

Weber, H., & Titzmann, P. (2003). Ärgerbezogene Reaktionen und Ziele: Entwicklung eines neuen Fragebogens [Anger-related reactions and goals: The development of a new Inventory]. *Diagnostica, 49*(3), 97–109. https://doi.org/10.1026/0012-1924.49.3.97

Weinberg, A., & Klonsky, E. D. (2009). Measurement of emotion dysregulation in adolescents. *Psychological Assessment, 21*(4), 616–621. https://doi.org/10.1037/a0016669

White, B. A., & Turner, K. A. (2014). Anger rumination and effortful control: Mediation effects on reactive but not proactive aggression. *Personality and Individual Differences, 56*, 186–189. https://doi.org/10.1016/j.paid.2013.08.012

Windle, M. (1992). Revised Dimensions of Temperament Survey (DOTS-R): Simultaneous group confirmatory factor analysis for adolescent gender groups. *Psychological Assessment, 4*(2), 228–234. https://doi.org/10.1037/1040-3590.4.2.228

Windle, M., & Lerner, R. M. (1986). Reassessing the dimensions of temperamental individuality across the life span: The Revised Dimensions of Temperament Survey (DOTS-R). *Journal of Adolescent Research, 1*(2), 213–229. https://doi.org/10.1177/074355488612007

Zeman, J., Shipman, K., & Penza-Clyve, S. (2001). Development and initial validation of the Children's Sadness Management Scale. *Journal of Nonverbal Behavior, 25*(3), 187–205. https://doi.org/10.1023/A:1010623226626

Zeman, J., Shipman, K., & Suveg, C. (2002). Anger and sadness regulation: Predictions to internalizing and externalizing symptoms in children. *Journal of Clinical Child and Adolescent Psychology, 31*(3), 393–398. https://doi.org/10.1207/153744202760082658

About the Authors

EVA L. FEINDLER, PhD, is professor of psychology at the Long Island University doctoral program in clinical psychology. As a faculty member of the concentration in high-risk family interventions and as former director of the doctoral program and the Psychological Services Center, she is directly involved in programs to help children and families manage their anger and resolve conflict.

She received her undergraduate degree in psychology from Mount Holyoke College and her graduate degrees from West Virginia University. Prior to her position at LIU, Dr. Feindler worked at Adelphi University, where she also directed the graduate program in applied behavioral technology. She has authored or edited several books—*Adolescent Anger Control: Cognitive-Behavioral Techniques; Adolescent Behavior Therapy Handbook; Assessment of Family Violence: A Handbook for Researchers and Practitioners;* and *Anger-Related Disorders: A Practitioner's Guide to Comparative Treatments*—as well as numerous articles on the assessment and treatment of parent and child anger. She has conducted training workshops across the United States and internationally.

She is featured on the *Aggression Replacement Training DVD* (Research Press), which presents the various components of aggression replacement training; she has also presented at APA, ABCT, and, most recently, SEPI conferences. In 2010 she completed a 2-year postgraduate program for relational psychotherapy at the Stephen Mitchell Relational Study Center in NYC, and in 2018 she completed a program at Widener University for advanced training in affirmative therapy for transgender communities. She is a fellow in Divisions 42 and 12 of APA and in ABCT.

GINA SITA-MOLZ, PsyD, BCBA, is a clinical psychologist and licensed behavior analyst specializing in helping
children and young adults with severe behavioral issues.
Dr. Sita-Molz earned her undergraduate degree in psychology from Boston University and received her doctoral degree in clinical psychology in 2012 from Long
Island University, C.W. Post Campus. She worked as
the director of psychology at a residential treatment
center for children with severe developmental disabilities before deciding to take time off to focus on raising

her three small children. She plans on opening a private practice in the coming year.
Dr. Sita-Molz and her family reside in Long Island, NY.